EVER AGAINST THE STREAM

The Politics of Karl Barth, 1906-1968

FRANK JEHLE

Translated by

Richard and Martha Burnett

William B. Eerdmans Publishing Company

Grand Rapids, Michigan / Cambridge, U.K.

First published in German under the title
Lieber unangenehm laut als angenehm leise
by Theologischer Verlag Zürich

English translation © 2002 Wm. B. Eerdmans Publishing Co.

Wm. B. Eerdmans Publishing Co.
255 Jefferson Ave. S.E., Grand Rapids, Michigan 49503 /
P.O. Box 163, Cambridge CB3 9PU U.K.

Printed in the United States of America

07 06 05 04 03 02   7 6 5 4 3 2 1

Library of Congress Cataloging-in-Publication Data

Jehle, Frank.
[Lieber unangenehm laut als angenehm leise. English]
Ever against the stream: the politics of Karl Barth, 1906-1968 /
Frank Jehle; translated by Richard and Martha Burnett.
p.   cm.
Includes bibliographical references (p.   ) and index.
ISBN 0-8028-4944-X (pbk.: alk. paper)
1. Barth, Karl, 1886-1968.   2. Europe — Politics and government — 20th century.
3. Christianity and politics — History — 20th century.   I. Title.

BX4827.B3 J3813   2002
261.7'092 — dc21

2002029679

www.eerdmans.com

EVER AGAINST THE STREAM

CONTENTS

ACKNOWLEDGMENTS

The book is a significantly revised and expanded version of a series of public lectures given at the University of St. Gallen in January 1999. I am grateful for the motivating interest of my listeners. Of equal importance to me was a group of very attentive students who attended a colloquium on Karl Barth that I organized a year earlier. My wife Marianne Jehle-Wildberger, Alfred Enz, Roland Kley, Henrique Schneider, and Wolfgang Kasprzik of the Theologischer Verlag Zürich helped me complete the manuscript. I thank them for their many ideas and suggestions. I also thank the administrators of the Karl Barth Nachlaß who, for almost three decades, with unprecedented devotion and erudition, have produced the various volumes of the *Gesamtausgabe*. Without them it would be impossible to publish such a book. Hopefully, this will help others take the research of Barth scholars seriously in other areas as well. I also wish to thank William B. Eerdmans, Jr., and Richard and Martha Burnett for this English edition.

St. Gallen   Frank Jehle

CHAPTER 1

_____

Introduction

Karl Barth died on December 10, 1968. Four days later, on December 14, a large group of mourners gathered to bid him farewell in the Basel cathedral. The occasion was broadcast on radio. *Not one* member of the Federal Council (i.e., the Swiss government) took part in the event, which was not the case with the funeral of the philosopher Karl Jaspers, who died only three months later. This bears witness to the tense relationship between the official Swiss government and the great theologian of Basel. The Federal Council had had difficulties with him for decades. During the war years, Federal Councilor Eduard von Steiger, who was minister of justice, illegally tapped Barth's telephone[1] and even considered whether he could put this troublesome man in jail.[2] Barth, for his part, made several critical statements about Bern (the capital of Switzerland), and particularly sharp statements toward the end of the Second World War when he grimly remarked that he too "had been responsible for and somehow had to share in the consequences of the mess that had been brought about by the Swiss authorities and how they had presented the face of Switzerland to the world."[3] In his opinion "the official face of Switzerland in those years was a much too smug one." "We behaved ourselves merely as Swiss . . . and

1. Busch, *Bogen,* p. 341.
2. Busch, *Bogen,* p. 357.
3. Barth, *Offene Briefe,* p. 17.

1

not as good Europeans. And precisely for that reason . . . we did not behave as truly good Swiss either."[4]

This statement shows that Barth identified with his homeland. He held the high ideal of a Switzerland that was open and humane. For him Switzerland was an integral part of Europe and bore a responsibility for the whole of Europe. According to Barth, it is *not* part of the nature of a state to "merely serve national interests." The God of Christian faith does "not only deal with *one* . . . state but with *his* state, the *just* state in *all* national states."[5] A Christian will "within his national state be on guard against everything; and, in case of an emergency, will protest against and resist all that cannot be reconciled to the character of a just state."[6] Without being intended as such, this sentence is a brilliant description of the role Barth played during the Second World War.

The governor of the canton of Basel-Stadt, Lukas Burckhardt, as the "highest" secular representative at the memorial service on December 14, 1968, said:

> Karl Barth was also a powerful political spirit, entirely of this world and . . . a great Swiss. . . . We must never forget that Karl Barth preached resistance — in Christian responsibility, yet in the plain language of the common man — against the evil of this world. In face of the threat of the Third Reich, when courage was lacking, he virtually embodied this resistance in his own person. Many believers were shocked, yet even more despondent folk regained courage, when Karl Barth, as a theologian and Christian, called for the use of arms for the righteous cause of the oppressed. During his lifetime, from the beginning when he was seen as the notorious "red pastor" of Safenwil up until his peculiar attitude toward aggressive Communism in Hungary, Karl Barth showed a non-conformist spirit in political matters and at times caused offence. And yet, it was perhaps this very quality that was so good for us.[7]

These words give at least some indication why the Swiss government sent none of its members to the memorial service. Barth was not a man

---

4. Barth, *Schweizer Stimme*, p. 368.
5. Barth, *Schweizer Stimme*, p. 275.
6. Barth, *Schweizer Stimme*, p. 276.
7. Barth, *Gedenkfeier*, pp. 33ff.

one could easily put to rest. He wrote to his colleague in Zürich, Emil Brunner, that whenever the church confesses, it "goes in fear and trembling against the stream and not with it."[8] Not only during the Second World War did Barth forfeit the favor of the Swiss government, but also in the fifties because of his — as Lukas Burckhardt discreetly put it — "peculiar attitude toward aggressive Communism." Barth's final revolt against the Federal Council happened in 1958 when he publicly opposed the idea of some military analysts who thought it necessary to provide Switzerland with nuclear arms.[9]

The story of Barth's relationship to his country could be described as an unhappy love story (at least in part). But his relationship to Germany after the war was also burdened with tensions. Because of critical statements addressed to the young *Bundesrepublik*, he was not honored with the peace prize of the German book trade union even though he had been nominated to receive it. In contrast to Barth, theologians like Albert Schweitzer, Romano Guardini, Martin Buber, Paul Tillich, Willem A. Visser 't Hooft, and Cardinal Augustin Bea received this important prize. Already in 1946, at a dinner in Bad Godesberg, Barth got into "an argument" with Konrad Adenauer. A "so-called 'Christian' party — and as such also a ruling party" was, for Barth, "in principle, an abomination."[10]

The history of Switzerland has special relevance today. People are going over the records again because many have realized that the traditional picture of Switzerland was not sufficiently scrutinized. Barth represents a *different* Switzerland than the one shown by members of the Federal Council such as Motta, Etter, von Steiger, and Pilet-Golaz. Barth is *also* part of the twentieth-century picture of Switzerland — and not merely some speck on a page. In a time when many no longer expected anything new from Christianity, he demonstrated that surprising consequences can come from *contemporaries who, on the basis of the Christian faith, are awake.* Because Barth sought to honor the "wholly Other," he had a broad perspective. Thus he *had to be* uncomfortable and *could* not conform.

---

8. Barth, *Offene Briefe,* p. 164.

9. Barth, *Offene Briefe,* pp. 398f.

10. *Carl Zuckmayer/Karl Barth, Späte Freundschaft in Briefen,* 11th ed. (Zürich: Theologischer Verlag Zürich, 1999), p. 31; ET, *A Late Friendship: The Letters of Karl Barth and Carl Zuckmayer,* trans. Geoffrey W. Bromiley (Grand Rapids: Eerdmans, 1982), p. 19.

The main goal of this book is to *tell* this story. Most of it does not need a great deal of explanation. The events speak for themselves. But Barth shall be quoted in detail in order that all readers will *hear* his unmistakably fresh voice. They should be able to form their own opinion. Barth was a brilliant speaker. It will become obvious as a central theme that Barth among other things was a great democrat. He wanted nothing to do with an authoritarian state that kept a close watch on its citizens, even though he was at times accused of totalitarian thinking.

We are already leaping ahead at this point to some important evidence from different decades: in his lectures on ethics in the spring of 1929, Barth *also* approved of — without any "if's" or "but's" — a democratic-type form of government for Germany. This was not something to be taken for granted in the national and international context of that time. The theological insight that the task and legitimacy of the state are dependent on God — or even more precisely: "on God's grace" — was the source for his statement that "fundamentally, even though in practice, in different ways," *all* are destined for political participation: "To be called 'by God's grace' [to act on behalf of the state] can neither be the responsibility of males alone, nor of one national constituency, nor of one rank or class within the state, nor of one single family or group of families to the exclusion of the rest of the members of the state. . . . Fundamentally, everyone is responsible for the actions of the state and is called to act within it." When Barth repeated this lecture in the fall semester of 1930/31 in Bonn, he added: "In this sense *all the power of the State comes from the people.*"[11]

Barth thus supported the right of women to vote. He opposed states characterized by rank or class, was against an inheritable monarchy (with the exception of a constitutional monarchy like the British one),[12] and was against a state in which *one* ethnic group would dominate others. And whoever holds a position of political leadership, as he elaborates in the same text, must measure himself according to the standard of whether he performs his office "in obedience to God or in service to his neighbor."[13]

In the spring of 1948, Barth was speaking at a student conference in

---

11. Barth, *Ethik II*, p. 338 (emphasis by Frank Jehle); ET, pp. 448-49 (revised).
12. See below, p. 6.
13. Barth, *Ethik II*, p. 339; ET, p. 449.

Hungary. He did not think the future "would be good if there was no longer room for a federal state under a constitution established by the freely educated and freely expressed will of the people, just like the Swiss confederation."[14] Barth would like to have exported the Swiss form of government to Eastern Europe. In the same speech he felt obliged to give further explanation, which possibly came as a surprise to some.

> Again and again there were people in the old days who could and wanted to think independently. It would not be good if such people would no longer exist in your generation. Listen to a few sentences by Immanuel Kant from his essay, "What is Enlightenment?" He says: "Enlightenment is the end of the immaturity of man which is his own fault. Immaturity is the inability to use one's own mind without the help of another person. This immaturity is one's own fault when its cause lies not with a deficiency of mind but with a lack of decision and courage to use one's mind without the help of someone else. *Sapere Aude!* Have the courage to make use of your own mind! This is therefore the motto of the Enlightenment." It would not be good if to-day's young people would no longer have an ear for the spirit that speaks from these sentences. It would be much better if the second-half of the twentieth century could become — if understood in the best sense — a time of such "Enlightenment," since the first-half has unexpectedly brought us such dark madness.[15]

Barth mentioned that this quotation from Kant on this occasion resulted in a "very clear sound of applause which was not entirely in accord with the program."[16] This passage is reminiscent of a later statement in the *Church Dogmatics* in which Barth calls the Holy Spirit the most intimate "friend of common sense."[17] To the extent that Barth followed the best traditions of the European Enlightenment, he took for granted that democracy — despite its weaknesses — is, relatively speaking, the "best" kind of state.

This book is written in chronological order. After these introductory thoughts and a survey of Barth as a theologian, it recalls the not-quite-

---

14. Barth, *Ungarnreise*, p. 13; ET, p. 60 (revised). See below, pp. 91-92.
15. Barth, *Ungarnreise*, pp. 12f.; ET, p. 60.
16. Busch, *Lebenslauf*, p. 367; ET, p. 354 (revised).
17. Barth, *KD* IV/4:31; *CD* IV/4:28 (revised).

twenty-year-old student of theology who in his student fraternity, with a fiery paper on the "social question," set foot on political ground for the first time. Another chapter follows on Barth's work as a pastor in Safenwil, where he became very involved with the suffering textile workers, helped set up labor unions, and became a member of the Social Democratic Party. The next two chapters deal with the two commentaries on the Epistle to the Romans and with the Church Struggle in Germany. Another part that has become especially relevant today deals with Barth's political debates after his forced return to Switzerland in 1935. He called for resistance against the National Socialist threat, which seemed — as already mentioned — to the official government of Switzerland as not diplomatic enough and too loud.

The next issue is the turbulent events after the Second World War: a new relationship to Germany, and Barth in the conflict zone of the Cold War between East and West. In the last chapter the theological background of Barth's political ethics will be considered. In his lectures "Justification and Justice" of 1938 and "The Christian Community and the Civil Community" of 1946, he shows that though the spiritual and political must be distinguished, there is a deep relationship between them. When the Weimar Republic faced its end, Barth said in a lecture that "only the clever English — perhaps one of the few nations truly gifted politically — foresaw in time the folly" of absolutism and "introduced checks" within its political system. Because of these "checks," Great Britain was spared "the catastrophe" (viz., totalitarianism).[18] Karl Barth was not only a great theologian. He was at the same time one of the most significant political and moral philosophers of the twentieth century.

18. Barth, *Prot. Theologie*, pp. 26f.; ET, p. 30.

CHAPTER 2

Karl Barth: The Theologian

The aim of this book is to single out a specific aspect of Karl Barth's life: his *political* life. It is necessary, however, to first give a survey of his life and work. His political engagement grows out of his theology. One can understand it only in the context of his biography.

Karl Barth (1886-1968) was the product of two Reformed theological dynasties. His mother, Anna Katharina Sartorius, was born in 1863. His father, Fritz Barth, was born in 1856 and was a professor of church history at the University of Bern. He was a member of the conservative wing of his church and began teaching in 1889. His son, Karl, began theological studies at the same university in the fall of 1904.

As was the custom in Switzerland at that time, Barth moved on to study at a German university after completing his basic courses in theology. After a sojourn in Berlin where he studied mainly with Adolf von Harnack and in Tübingen where, according to his father's will, he listened "with considerable resentment"[1] to the conservative, biblical theologian Adolf Schlatter, he came to Marburg, which was dominated by neo-Kantianism. In retrospect, the summer semester of 1908 was the most important one to him. Wilhelm Herrmann, whose classes on dogmatics (i.e., the doctrine of faith) and ethics he attended, was "*the* theological teacher" of his student years.[2] After his final exams in theology

1. Busch, *Lebenslauf,* p. 55; ET, p. 43.
2. Busch, *Lebenslauf,* p. 49; ET, p. 44.

and his ordination, which was officiated by his own father on November 4, 1908, in the Bern Münster church, Barth became the assistant of Marburg professor Martin Rade for two semesters and helped him primarily with the editing of what was, at the time, the leading Protestant journal, *Christliche Welt*.

A few brief details about the most important professors just mentioned: Harnack was generally thought of as the most famous Protestant theologian at the turn of the century. As professor of New Testament and church history, he researched the origins of Christian dogma in closest detail. No one knew the history of the early church and its development better than he. In his book *The Essence of Christianity: Sixteen Lectures for Students of All Faculties Delivered in the University of Berlin during the Winter Semester of 1899-1900*, he developed a powerful overview of Christianity. As he himself said, he wanted to present Christianity "solely according to its historical meaning," which meant "by the methods of historical science and the experience of life gained by history relived."[3] Barth put almost all his energy into Harnack's seminar during his semester at Berlin (he often refused to go to the theater, which he found so fascinating, because he spent most of his time behind books in order to satisfy his famous teacher). As a result, he absorbed the entire art of the science of history as it had developed to maturity throughout the nineteenth century. Even in the final volumes of his *Church Dogmatics*, it is clear how much Barth profited from Harnack. Barth, for example, owes the title of one paragraph of the *Church Dogmatics*, "The Life of the Children of God,"[4] to a conversation he had in 1925 with his old and, even then, still-much-admired teacher.

"To me, historical critics must be *more critical*."[5] This famous sentence in the preface to the second edition of his Romans commentary of 1922 was written by someone who knew what he was talking about. Barth worked all his life with the tools of historical criticism. The transmission of texts must be carefully analyzed. One must test their credibility and weigh differences between partly contradictory traditions. Barth

3. Adolf von Harnack, *Das Wesen des Christentums* (Leipzig: Hinrichs'sche Buchhandlung, 1900), p. 4; ET, *What Is Christianity?* trans. Thomas Bailey Saunders (New York: G. P. Putnam's Sons, 1901), p. 6 (revised).

4. Barth, *KD* I/2:397f.; *CD* I/2:362f.; regarding the title, see *KD* I/2:403f.; *CD* I/2:367f.

5. Barth, *Römerbrief 2*, p. xii (p. xviii).

did not want to do away with historical criticism. He wanted rather to outdo it. His "entire attention [was] directed toward looking *through* the historical to the spiritual dimension of the Bible."[6] As one who wanted to understand, he sought to come to the point where he stood before "the mystery of the *subject matter*" and not merely "before the mystery of the *document*."[7] He did not want to omit historical work in the stricter sense of this word. But to him it served only as a preparation for the much more important process of a serious and reverent[8] understanding — and indeed, *not* only with respect to the Bible. Barth also explicitly insisted that he would apply his method to "Lao-Tse or Goethe."[9]

Other important teachers were the Marburg professors Herrmann and Rade, who represented the dominant, liberal, "free-thinking world of Protestantism" of that day.[10] Barth learned from Wilhelm Herrmann that it is impossible within the realm of Christian faith to develop a theology without far-reaching ethical implications. Martin Rade was a fatherly friend to the young Barth and for decades followed the course of his life and work with great interest. On August 20, 1909, Barth wrote a letter to Rade and said that his work and stay in Rade's home had been "*the* highlight of his years of travel." The *Christliche Welt* had been for him an "introduction into the life of the Christian world." With his "transition from university to praxis," he said he could not have asked for a better experience and wished that "every young theologian could have such an experience."[11]

From September 1909 to June 1911 Barth worked as an assistant pastor in the German-speaking congregation in Geneva, where he got to know Adolf Keller and John R. Mott, two leaders of the ecumenical movement. Keller demonstrated his ecumenical interest "by joining in the work of the World Alliance for Promoting International Friendship Through the Churches and as the secretary of the Federation of Swiss

6. Barth, *Römerbrief* 2, p. v (p. xi). The same quotation is found in more detail on p. 11.

7. Barth, *Römerbrief* 2, p. xii (p. xix).

8. Barth, *Römerbrief* 2, p. xiii (p. xix).

9. Barth, *Römerbrief* 2, p. xv (p. xiii).

10. Compare Johannes Rathje, *Die Welt des freien Protestantismus. Ein Beitrag zur deutsch-evangelischen Geistesgeschichte. Dargestellt am Leben und Werk Martin Rades* (Stuttgart: Klotz, 1952).

11. Barth-Rade, p. 65.

Protestant Churches, and the American Federal Council."[12] In 1895 Mott founded the World Student Christian Federation, and from 1915 on he served as the general secretary of the Young Men's Christian Association. In 1910 he organized the first world missions conference in Edinburgh. Thus, from very early on, Barth had close contact to the growing ecumenical movement.

During his time in Geneva, Barth became acquainted with his future wife, Nelly Hoffmann (1893-1976), who was a member of his confirmation class. Out of consideration for Barth, Nelly gave up her life's plan to study the violin. The couple had one daughter, Franziska, and four sons: Markus, Christoph, Matthias, and Hans Jakob.

From 1911 to 1921 Barth was the pastor of a congregation in Safenwil, Aargau, which consisted mostly of farmers and working-class people. He took his professional duties very seriously. He felt it was important during that time to become a member of the religious socialist movement as it was then represented in Switzerland, with different emphases, by Leonhard Ragaz and Hermann Kutter. Both appealed to Christoph Blumhardt the younger (1842-1919).[13] At first it seemed that Barth was especially close to Ragaz. The young pastor was very practically involved in the labor union movement. Later he became more closely aligned to Kutter and his emphasis on preaching as more important than specific political work. But during the battles of the thirties he became once again closer (not personally, but with respect to the issues at hand) to Ragaz, who clearly stood out in his negative assessment of National Socialism. Another very important person was Eduard Thurneysen, who served at that time as the pastor of another congregation in Aargau. Throughout his life he was Barth's closest and most devoted friend.

The decisive turning point in Barth's life took place during the First World War. Its terrors caused Barth to lose faith in liberal theology's belief in progress (and also religious socialism, to the extent that it sought to establish God's kingdom on earth). Between July 1916 and August 1918, Barth worked on his first great commentary on the Epistle to the Romans. Postdated 1919, a thousand copies were published in Bern dur-

12. *Die Religion in Geschichte und Gegenwart* 3, 3rd ed. (Tübingen: J. C. B. Mohr, 1959), p. 1236.

13. See below, pp. 25-26.

ing the Christmas season of 1918. A detailed review in the *Christliche Welt* written by Adolf Jülicher, a prominent professor of New Testament, is one among other reasons why the book caused such a sensation. Jülicher charged that the book was not "scientific." Barth's preface contains the following, famously provocative sentences:

> The historical critical method of biblical research has its place; it points to a preparation for understanding that is never superfluous. But if I had to choose between it and the old doctrine of inspiration, I would resolutely choose the latter. It has a greater, deeper, more important place because it points directly to the task of understanding, without which all preparation is worthless. I am happy that I do not have to choose between the two. But my entire attention has been directed toward looking *through* the historical to the spiritual dimension of the Bible, where we find the eternal Spirit. What was once a serious matter is still serious today.[14]

These words raised suspicion among members of the *older* generation, such as Harnack, that Barth was a pietistic enthusiast [*Schwärmer*], whereas some members of the *younger* generation (among them Friedrich Gogarten and Emil Brunner, and a little later, Rudolf Bultmann, with the second, thoroughly revised edition of 1922) enthusiastically hailed Barth's commentary on Romans as the manifesto of a new theological epoch.

One consequence of the first edition was that Barth was called to the University of Göttingen to be an honorary professor of Reformed theology at the beginning of the winter semester of 1921/22. The second edition of the *Römerbrief*, which he thoroughly revised while still in Safenwil, became a best-seller and is still often reprinted. An entire generation of theologians as well as nontheologians has grown up with it. Many phrases of the book's second edition, also strongly influenced by Kierkegaard and Dostoyevsky, became popular: faith is an "impossible possibility," an "empty space," a "bombshell crater." Revelation is an event "vertically from above."[15] Like others before him, such as Luther and Pascal, Barth loved paradoxical statements: "As theologians we

14. Barth, *Römerbrief* 2, p. v (p. xi).

15. Such statements are repeated again and again in the second edition of Barth's *Römerbrief* commentary.

should speak about God. But we are human beings and as such are not able to speak about God. We should know the difference between what we should do and what we cannot do, and at precisely this point, give God the praise."[16] These sentences are found in Barth's programmatic lecture of October 1922, "The Word of God and the Task of Theology." Because of its peculiar vocabulary, one outsider at the time coined the expression "dialectical theology" (in America, a "theology of crisis") to characterize the work of Barth and his friends during the twenties. The mouthpiece of this group of theologians was a newly founded journal called *Zwischen den Zeiten* (i.e., *Between the Times*). In a later chapter of this book, we will deal more specifically with both of Barth's commentaries on the Epistle to the Romans.

While in Göttingen, Münster (beginning in 1925), and Bonn (beginning in 1930), Barth applied himself to his new role as an academician. At first, in addition to his courses in theology, he held seminars on New Testament exegesis and church history. But his leanings toward systematic theology (i.e., dogmatics *and* ethics) became more and more evident. He approached the task of writing a dogmatics with several false starts (at first in lectures and then in book form). In 1927 the first volume of *Christian Dogmatics in Outline: The Doctrine of the Word of God* appeared. Instead of continuing with a second volume, Barth started over again, having been impressed by the early medieval theologian Anselm of Canterbury, whom he published a monograph on in 1931 entitled *Fides quaerens intellectum*.[17] From 1932 to 1967, the thirteen monumental volumes of the *Church Dogmatics* were published, though the work itself remains incomplete. The new title emphasizes that Barth pursued theology as an *ecclesiastical* science, which he had learned to do, in spite of all their differences, from Friedrich Schleiermacher, his highly respected "nemesis." Schleiermacher (1768-1834) was the most famous Protestant theologian of the nineteenth century. In his *Brief Outline of Theology as a Field of Study*, he had defined theology as an *ecclesiastical* science. According to him, theology falls apart without reference to the church. Each of its individual disciplines comes under "the science to which

16. Barth, *Kl. Arbeiten* 3, p. 151.

17. Karl Barth, *Fides quaerens intellectum. Anselms Beweis der Existenz Gottes im Zusammenhang seines theologischen Programms* (1931), ed. Eberhard Jüngel and Ingolf U. Dalferth (Zürich: Theologischer Verlag, 1981); ET, *Anselm: Fides Quaerens Intellectum* (London: SCM Press, 1960).

they belong according to their content": "the art of language and the art of history, . . . the doctrine of the soul and the doctrine of ethics, in addition to those disciplines deriving from them."[18]

During the twenties Barth's life appeared to be outwardly quiet. He rose gradually to become the most highly regarded professor of theology in Germany. His situation fundamentally changed, however, when Adolf Hitler came to power on January 30, 1933. Some young people who no longer remembered Barth's religious socialist moorings in Safenwil found his political attitude surprising. At a time when many were cheering the führer uncritically, and even some clergymen believed that Hitler was Christ returned, Barth produced in the summer of 1933 a pugnacious pamphlet entitled *Theological Existence Today!* With cool but biting irony, he said he would "endeavor to go on working with his students in Bonn, doing theology and nothing but theology, now as before, as if nothing had ever happened. With perhaps a slightly raised tone, but without direct allusions: something like the chanting of the hours by the Benedictines nearby in the Maria Laach, which would go on undoubtedly without break or interruption even in the Third Reich," he vowed to press on.[19] When he refused to take the obligatory, unconditional oath of allegiance to the führer, after a rather long criminal proceeding, he was "put into retirement" on June 21, 1935. For all practical purposes, he was no longer allowed to be a professor. Only three days later the government of the canton of Basel-Stadt quickly resolved to establish and call Barth to a new teaching position at the university of his hometown, where he worked throughout the last three decades of his life.

Until he was expelled from Germany, Barth worked as a theological counselor to the Confessing Church and drafted his most important contribution, the Theological Declaration of Barmen, which was ratified on May 31, 1934. This document not only provides a summary of Barth's theology, but had and continues to have more influence upon the theological discussion of the entire ecumenical movement than any other document of the twentieth century. The first thesis states: "Jesus

18. Friedrich Schleiermacher, *Kurze Darstellung des theologischen Studiums*, ed. Heinrich Scholz (Leipzig, 1910; Hildesheim, 1961), p. 3; ET, *Brief Outline of Theology as a Field of Study*, trans. Terrence N. Tice (Lewiston, N.Y.: Edwin Mellen Press, 1990), p. 4 (revised).

19. Fürst, *Scheidung*, p. 43; ET, p. 9 (revised).

Christ, as he is attested for us in Holy Scripture, is the one Word of God which we have to hear and which we have to trust and obey in life and in death. — We reject the false doctrine, as though the church could and would have to acknowledge as a source of its proclamation, apart from and besides this one Word of God, still other events and powers, figures and truths, as God's revelation."[20] This first thesis, with its strict focus upon the exclusiveness of God's revelation in Jesus Christ, contradicted the pseudoreligious claims of various political and civic ideologies. When Emil Brunner of Zürich, who was himself considered a dialectical theologian during the twenties, stood gently but resolutely against the severity of Barth's approach in his work *Nature and Grace*, Barth hurled at him probably his most polemical pamphlet of all: *No! An Answer to Emil Brunner* (both publications came out in 1934).[21] Those who up until then had not suspected a breakup even after 1933 when *Zwischen den Zeiten* was no longer published, finally recognized that the group of dialectical theologians had completely fallen apart. Barth, Brunner, Bultmann, and Gogarten each went his own way. For a while Gogarten even became a member of the "German Christians," a group sympathetic to Hitler. Yet even though the debates in the fifties over "demythologizing" seemed to overshadow Barth's personal friendship with Bultmann, which began during his studies in Marburg, they nevertheless remained friends, in spite of their theological differences, especially during the Church Struggle. Neither Barth nor Bultmann can be understood apart from an awareness of their close affinities and mutual sympathies throughout each decade of their lives.

During the Second World War, Barth concentrated on his academic lectures in Basel, which remained the indissoluble link to the gradual growth of the *Church Dogmatics*. Contrary to what one might think, the *Church Dogmatics* is thoroughly related to the present. It is remarkable that — *at least superficially considered* — *Barth very often sought to relate to his day and time by contradicting it:* During a time of general enthusiasm for Hitler and for a revelation of God in the "national spirit," he said "No!" During the forties, when many cities in Europe were reduced to rubble and countless people were discouraged, Barth described, in a volume of his *Church Dogmatics* published in 1945, the "Creation as Bene-

---

20. Book of Confessions, p. 257.
21. Fürst, *Scheidung*, pp. 169f. and 208f.

fit" *(Wohltat)*.[22] In a further volume of 1951, he took up Albert Schweitzer's phrase "respect for life."[23] The same thinker who in his Romans commentary called God "wholly Other," in 1956 published a work entitled *The Humanity of God*,[24] and in the same year sang the praises of Mozart.[25] How Barth sought to relate to his day and time by contradicting it is also seen in the fact that he, the famous polemicist against National Socialism, did not allow himself to be taken in by anti-Communism during the Cold War. But from his correspondence with Reformed Hungarian bishop Albert Bereczky and Czech theologian Josef L. Hromadka, we also know that he *simultaneously* warned his friends of an all-too-compliant accommodation of Communism.

After the Second World War, Barth became one of the dominant figures of the ecumenical movement. His impact on the French- and English-speaking worlds, and on the Roman Catholic world, grew ever larger and culminated in his trip to America in 1962 and in his visit with Pope Paul VI in the fall of 1966. Shortly before, he concluded his teaching career in the winter semester of 1961/62 with his lecture "Evangelical Theology: An Introduction."[26] During his lifetime it was already difficult to have an overview of all the literature written about him. Some of the best works were written in foreign languages and by Roman Catholic authors such as Hans Urs von Balthasar,[27] Hans Küng,[28] and Henri Bouillard.[29] Although he was frail in his final years, Barth remained ac-

22. Barth, *KD* III/1:377f.; *CD* III/1:330f.

23. Barth, *KD* III/4:366f.; *CD* III/4:324f.

24. Karl Barth, *Die Menschlichkeit Gottes* (Zürich: Evangelischer Verlag, 1956); ET, *The Humanity of God*, trans. John Newton Thomas (Richmond: John Knox, 1960).

25. Karl Barth, *Wolfgang Amadeus Mozart 1756/1956*, 13th ed. (Zürich: Theologischer Verlag, 1996); ET, *Wolfgang Amadeus Mozart, 1756/1956*, trans. Clarence K. Pott (Grand Rapids: Eerdmans, 1956).

26. Karl Barth, *Einführung in die evangelische Theologie* (Zürich: Evangelischer Verlag, 1962); ET, *Evangelical Theology: An Introduction*, trans. Grover Foley (New York: Holt, Rinehart, and Winston, 1963).

27. Hans Urs von Balthasar, *Karl Barth. Darstellung und Deutung seiner Theologie* (1951), 4th ed. (Einsiedeln: Johannes Verlag, 1976); ET, *The Theology of Karl Barth*, trans. John Drury (New York: Holt, Rinehart, and Winston, 1971).

28. Hans Küng, *Rechtfertigung. Die Lehre Karl Barths und eine katholische Besinnung* (Einsiedeln: Johannes Verlag, 1957); ET, *Justification: The Doctrine of Karl Barth and a Catholic Reflection* (Philadelphia: Westminster, 1981).

29. Henri Bouillard, *Karl Barth. Genèse et évolution de la théologie dialectique* (Paris: Aubier/Editions Montaigne, 1957).

tive to the very end. On the eve of his death he was working on a manuscript for a lecture he wanted to give in January 1969 before a mixed Protestant and Roman Catholic audience on the occasion of the Ecumenical Week of Prayer for the Unity of Christendom.

Reflecting on Barth's entire life's work, one notices an *increasing focus upon the doctrine of Christ*. Barth meditated more and more intensely on the incarnation of God in Jesus of Nazareth and its implications. His three volumes (2,984 pages in all) on the doctrine of reconciliation are, in the stricter sense, the highlight of the *Church Dogmatics*. The focus upon the doctrine of Christ, paradoxically, made it possible for Barth to take many excursions into a surprising number of areas. In his work we find, for example, extensive sections on Friedrich Nietzsche and Jean-Paul Sartre, on Leibniz and Lessing. In his book *Protestant Theology in the Nineteenth Century* of 1947, which was based upon lectures given from 1932 to 1933, he — differently than what one might expect reading the title — deals with, among other things: Rousseau, Kant, Herder, Novalis, Hegel, etc. The chapter on Hegel, for example, is acclaimed as especially brilliant by Hegel specialists.

On the one hand, since his Romans commentary, it was theologically characteristic of Barth to focus on the Bible (some of the most impressive parts of the *Church Dogmatics* are his penetrating excursuses on, for example, the book of Job). On the other hand, he also meticulously worked through the theological tradition from ancient times (a task for which, from 1929 on, his friend and coworker Charlotte von Kirschbaum [1899-1975] independently and indispensably helped and supported him). Since his book on Anselm of Canterbury of 1931, Barth gave himself more and more to studying the theological thinkers of the ancient and medieval church, also to the works of Protestant orthodoxy, which made it possible for him to offer in his prolegomenon to the *Church Dogmatics* a pioneering contribution to the doctrine of the Trinity. His theological-historical excursus on the doctrine of predestination in the *Church Dogmatics* is of monographic proportion. Barth's major theological works do not shy away from the most subtle definitions and are surrounded by an almost inestimable amount of pamphlets and brochures in which he often took positions regarding issues of the day. *It is this aspect which lies at the center of this book.*

In 1968, shortly before his death, Barth was honored by the German Academy for Speech and Poetry in Darmstadt with the Sigmund Freud

Prize for scientific prose. This says something about his use of language. We are faced here with a double-sided phenomenon: Stylistically, his academic works are characteristically circular and partly redundant. The Dutch theologian Kornelis Heiko Miskotte talks about "the principle of repetition, execution, and internal connection in the flow of inexhaustible eloquence" of Barth's prose. It is the attempt to use terms which are not, strictly speaking, suitable for the task, in service of a "multi-dimensional truth which is never simply 'given.'"[30] In more popular contexts (also in the prefaces to his books and in his letters), Barth shows himself to be a brilliant rhetorician who loves to play with language in order to make penetrating, often ironical points.

30. Kornelis Heiko Miskotte, *Über Karl Barths Kirchliche Dogmatik. Kleine Präludien und Phantasien* (Munich: Kaiser, 1961), p. 18.

CHAPTER 3

"Zofingia and the Social Question"

pg 21

From his earliest semesters, the young Barth was fascinated with theology. His seminar papers[1] show us a student who from the very beginning was clearly focused on going his own way. But now to the actual topic of this book, the *political* Karl Barth. As a theology student — not yet even twenty years old — Barth was concerned not only about "pure theology" but also about issues of his day. His membership, beginning in the fall of 1904, in the Swiss Zofinger Union of Bern — which, as a fraternity, was called the "Zofingia" — was important to him. He even presided over it in the summer semester of 1906. The Zofingia was the place where Barth, for the first time, stepped on political ground.

The Zofinger Union was founded in 1819 and was Switzerland's oldest student union. It was a spiritual offspring of the German Student Fraternity, which, two years after the famous festival in Wartburg to celebrate Reformation on October 18-19, 1817, had been banned by the reactionary forces of Europe under the leadership of Prince Metternich. The fraternity demanded "a constitutional monarchy with ministerial responsibility, the rights of: public assembly, trial by jury, freedom of speech and press, self-government, universal military conscription, etc. Radical groups wanted a republic."[2]

---

1. Barth, *Kl. Arbeiten* 1.
2. *Meyers Grosses Taschenlexikon* 4 (Mannheim, Leipzig, Vienna, and Zürich: BI-Taschenbuchverlag, 1995), p. 142.

Nous l'avions bâtie,
la blanche maison
où coula notre vie
dans sa belle saison. . . .
Amis, bon courage
bravons leur courroux!
Dieu bénit notre ouvrage
et triomphe avec nous.[3]

This song, still sung today at each meeting of the Zofingia as one rises to one's feet, is the French version of a song by August von Binzer which was sung by the outraged students on November 26, 1819, in Jena on the occasion of the forced dissolution of the fraternity:

We had built
a magnificent house
and in it we trusted in God
in spite of weather, storm and terror. . . .
The house may fall apart,
what problem is that?
The spirit lives in all of us
and God is our fortress![4]

One could almost define the Zofingia as the liberal wing of the German Student Fraternity transported into Switzerland, including its French-speaking regions. Students from Zürich and Bern met and celebrated to-gether from July 21 to 24, 1819, in the small town of Zofingen (Aargau), which was approximately halfway between their universities. "During their negotiations in the restaurants, 'The Ox' ['Ochsen'] and 'The Horse' ['Rössli'], all those present were filled with a not clearly defined and therefore all-the-more-fiery-excitement."[5] The decision was made to have this meeting annually. Students from other towns in Switzerland soon joined. So-called sections developed in Zürich and Bern (1819), Lausanne and Luzern (1820), Basel and Freiburg im Breisgau (1821), St.

3. *Zofinger Liederbuch*, 1969 ed. (Bern, 1969), p. 4.

4. Ernst Ludwig Schellenberg, *Das deutsche Volkslied* 2 (Berlin, 1916), p. 477.

5. Werner Kundert and Ulrich Im Hof, in *Der schweizerische Zofingerverein 1819-1969* (Bern: K. J. Wyss Erben AG, 1969), p. 27. The parenthetical page references in the following paragraphs are to this work.

Gallen and Schaffhausen (1824), Chur (1828), Freiburg im Üechtland (1829), Aarau (1834), Lugano (1854), and Schwyz (1857) (p. 416). The places named make it very clear that from the beginning there were not only university students but also high school students represented in the Zofingia. Already in 1820 the Zofinger Union had 120 members from four different cantons (p. 28). The basic thought was that all Swiss citizens striving for higher education should be gathered into a single union. In the long run, however, this goal was not to be realized. Already in 1824 the bishop of Basel, Franz Xaver de Neveu, announced that the "unfortunate alliance" of students from Solothurn with the "organization of Protestants from Zofingen" deeply grieved his "heart as a spiritual leader" all the more because the purpose of these organizations was nothing less than the "undermining and the revolutionization of church and state." Students of Roman Catholic theology "who were involved in a secret society, and with Protestants," could not be ordained (p. 30).

It is not necessary to give further details. The Swiss Zofinger Union developed into a union where Roman Catholics are still an exception. During the course of the nineteenth century, further divisions took place. The following question became paramount: Did they want to identify with a certain political party (as the "Helvetia" — the most important branch that broke away from the Zofingia — did in supporting the "Radicals"), or did they want to remain open to go in different directions? In 1848 the following sentence was accepted into its bylaws: "As a free school of free conviction, the Zofinger Union accepts all opinions" (p. 57). Members of Zofingia were convinced that their organization could not exclude any political perspective (p. 57). The spectrum of the Zofingia was broad.

Having engaged in political discourse for years, the Zofinger Union was "in its outer and inner structure a mirror of the intellectual life of the Swiss people and of the Swiss state, where church and theology had to fulfill their tasks not in separation but in *critical* solidarity."[6] Many important Swiss Protestant theologians in the nineteenth century and at the turn of the century were members of the Zofingia. Karl Barth was an enthusiastic, even if rebellious, member. He maintained membership in the organization up until his latter years. Even in 1959 he was twice invited by the active Basel group to join them for an evening of discussion.[7] Looking back,

---

6. Andreas Lindt, in *Der schweizerische Zofingerverein 1819-1969*, p. 203.
7. Barth, *Gespräche* 1, pp. 5ff. and 44ff. See below, pp. 90-91.

he said he had "spent his days in Bern in the glory of a student."[8] We have to smile as we read a section of the autobiography of the German theologian Günther Dehn (during the time of the German Church Struggle and later, a very close personal friend of Barth), who describes his first encounter with his future comrade in battle in the following way:

> We were invited for dinner at the home of Fritz Barth, Professor of Church History and New Testament in Bern. I sat next to his oldest son, a theology student. I would have liked to have had a conversation with him regarding the situation of the church and theology, particularly in Switzerland, but there was no opportunity to do so. He certainly talked enough, but it was always about his organization, the "Zofingia," which made me especially angry since I was a sworn enemy of student organizations. He obviously had had several debates during the semester and was full of all his experiences. It was entirely concealed from me that night that this student should later become the famous theologian, Karl Barth.[9]

When Barth was an active member of the Zofingia, some members were engaged in the *religious socialist movement* which was popular at the time. Hermann Kutter and Leonhard Ragaz, the two "leaders" of the religious-socialist movement, were members of the Zofingia and published articles in the *Centralblatt* of the Swiss Zofinger Union. In 1889, when Ragaz was a student in Basel, he asked the Zofingia to "study the social question," which is "the highest matter" that moves "our imaginatively lack-luster day."[10]

For Barth research it is fortunate that Barth's lecture "Zofingia and the Social Question," which he gave in the Zofingia of Bern on January 20, 1906, has survived. His debates in the Zofingia, mentioned by Dehn, were related to this lecture. At the time Barth was in his third semester and was not quite twenty years old. Yet it is obvious that he was not only a highly intellectually gifted young student, he was also, at the same time, fully awake politically. One fascinating detail about this lecture of the young Barth is that among his listeners was also the future federal councilor and

8. Barth, *Gespräche* 2, p. 533.

9. Günther Dehn, *Die alte Zeit — die vorigen Jahre. Lebenserinnerungen* (Munich: Kaiser, 1962), p. 143.

10. *Der schweizerische Zofingerverein 1819-1969*, p. 203.

minister of justice Eduard von Steiger, whom Barth had a falling out with in the forties, mainly regarding the question of refugees. From the record of the meeting we learn that the two did not get along well even then.

Barth was a serious and sensible young man, though he could at times, in certain social settings, get carried away. In his lecture he criticized his organization by making it clear to his fellow students that only sons coming from good homes could afford membership in the Zofingia. The membership fee and additional expenses were high (ten francs per month), more than twice what factory workers at that time were earning in a thirteen- to fifteen-hour day.[11] To Barth this was not in accord with the original concern of the founders of the Zofinger Union. Demographically, not everything was "as it should be." Barth charged that the number of "Swiss students from lower, middle-class circles" in the Zofingia was, relatively speaking, rather small.

> And yet it would be among the higher tasks of the Zofingia . . . — especially given its [present] make-up — to work towards bridging the social gap. I can make allowance for a few exceptions but, in general, we have to admit that we are well on the way to becoming *a student association of the "good society."* . . . but if the Zofingia becomes a clique and, in fact, a clique of the "good society" then a social activity at its center, i.e. the social education of its members . . . , is seriously at risk, and even brought to a standstill, because the "Zofingia" itself has then become an accomplice in the social struggle.[12]

Barth's main concern was "the very ordinary question of the money bag" (p. 86). The "official and unofficial burden" of members would have "to be reduced at all costs" (p. 87). Barth insisted that they make room for "greater social variety within the make-up of the union." Furthermore, he demanded that "the old emphasis on class distinction be abolished" (p. 90).

The political acumen of the young Barth's lecture is impressive. During the first part of his exposition, he spoke in detail about the statistical successes of the Social Democratic Party in the German Reich, which indicated to him that the party was addressing the social problems of the day:

11. See below, p. 26.
12. Barth, *Kl. Arbeiten* 1, pp. 85f. The parenthetical page references in the following text are to this work.

I am reminding you of . . . familiar things when I quote, for example, several statistical results from the German *Reichstag election* of 1903: In Saxony in 1903 there were 22 Social Democrats elected from a group of 23 representatives, 18 of them elected on the first ballot. In the Hanseatic cities of Lübeck, Bremen and Hamburg, the vote was entirely Social Democratic: of 220,000 votes, 136,000 went to the Social Democratic Party. Berlin, the capital of the Reich, elected 5 Social Democrats out of 6 representatives! Cities like Munich, Stuttgart, Karlsruhe, Weimar, Braunschweig, Speyer, Nuremberg, Mannheim, Darmstadt, Mainz, Esslingen and others, as well as several small Thuringian principalities, voted typically throughout according to Social Democratic principles. — These are merely names and numbers, but I think the language they speak is clear! (p. 73)

He also talked about Switzerland and emphasized that since 1906, "the situation was more and more" intense, that the "split between *capital* and *work*, between *Mammonism* and *pauperism*, in short, between *rich* and *poor*, was growing — whether such was stated by social democratic agitators or not" (p. 74).

Even at that time Barth was speaking about the "unbearable militarism" of Germany and about the "Byzantine principality" and "Cossack terror" of Russia (p. 73). He quoted from a 1905 sermon by Leonhard Ragaz delivered at the Basel cathedral where Ragaz served as pastor:

The social debate has erupted all along the way. It has taken on enormous intensity. To our national embarrassment, it has even lately come to violent disturbance of our civic order. Deep bitterness has taken over minds. Our people are threatening to split into two enemy camps, just as in the worst times of our history. And if it happens that a well-armed military shall walk the streets of our cities, we shall then see before our eyes the specter of a bloody civil war. On both sides, the [current] battle manifests things that are hurting us and are prophetic of nothing good. More and more, the movement impinges upon all circumstances; many see their outward existence as threatened, others suffer from inward conflicts provoked by this situation. (p. 74)[13]

13. As quoted in Leonhard Ragaz, *Busse und Glauben. Bettagspredigt, gehalten am 17. Sept. 1905 im Münster zu Basel* (Basel, 1905), pp. 7f.

Ragaz had caused a great stir and threw the entire city into an uproar when he preached in 1903 in the context of the Basel bricklayers' strike. He attacked "official Christendom" as "cold and uncomprehending" with respect to "building a new world." From his standpoint, Christians should be "on the side of the poor and developing classes."[14] The young Barth from the very beginning was considerably influenced by Ragaz.

As a student of theology, Barth certainly also knew how to quote the Bible. He recalled the twofold law of love, Luke 10:28f., and interpreted it, in the theological jargon of the day, as "the responsibility of the individual to respect the divine, on the one hand, and humanity, on the other." And finally, one other important motive regarding Barth's lifework: If already as a young student he chose the "social question" as a central theme, he did so purposely following the tradition of the Swiss Reformation. He appealed to Zwingli, Oecolampadius (the Basel Reformer), and Calvin. With a certain sense of satisfaction, he emphasized that "the principle of equality of all citizens was well-known in the Swiss city-republics, like Basel and Zürich, long before the French Revolution."[15]

The young theologian thus knew that Swiss Protestantism had a specific political dimension. From the very beginning there was a special affinity between Reformed Christendom and republican sentiment. Historically, it is more than simply a coincidence that "the political form of representative Democracy" goes back to, among other things, the "basic principle of the division of offices" in the "ecclesial ordinances" of John Calvin.[16] Those in 1906 who got to know the young Zofinger Karl Barth had reason to be curious about his future path within the political realm.

14. Markus Mattmüller, *Leonhard Ragaz und der religiöse Sozialismus. Die Entwicklung der Persönlichkeit und des Werkes bis ins Jahr 1913* (Basel and Stuttgart: Helbing und Lichtenhahn, 1957), pp. 84f.

15. Barth, *Kl. Arbeiten* 1, p. 76.

16. Christian Link, in *Calvin-Studienausgabe, 2, Gestalt und Ordnung der Kirche* (Neukirchen-Vluyn: Neukirchener Verlag, 1997), p. vi.

CHAPTER 4

Pastor in Safenwil

On July 9, 1911, Karl Barth was installed as minister of the congregation of Safenwil-Aargau. He was twenty-five years old. Parishioners immediately came to know him as a pastoral counselor who cared not only about their souls but also about their bodily existence. Young Barth was a "religious socialist" minister who had been inspired by Leonhard Ragaz and Hermann Kutter and also by Christoph Blumhardt the younger. This latter theologian from Württemberg had joined the Social Democratic Party in the fall of 1899. At the time, such a move was very unusual and caused a great sensation. According to the wishes of church authorities, Blumhardt had to "voluntarily" give up his title as a minister. On December 18, 1900, he was elected into the state parliament of Württemberg as a Social Democratic representative, where he remained a member for six years. Among the theologians at the turn of the century who publicly took the side of the suffering working-class, Blumhardt was probably the "greatest" and most courageous. Barth met the famous, or rather infamous, man on December 27, 1907, and paid him several visits from that day on.[1] After his death in 1919, Barth wrote an obituary in which he testified that Blumhardt was someone "with a fine and penetrating ear to hear those sighing for redemption." This sigh goes throughout the entire creation. Blumhardt could not simply accept that "which is, which endures, and which is valid now." The "burden . . .

---

1. Busch, *Lebenslauf,* p. 55; ET, pp. 43-44 (revised).

and also the joy" of his life consisted in believing "always and everywhere in the new that waits to be born out of the old."[2] Barth was convinced that Blumhardt "would remain alive for all who could understand what his life was about: the victory of the future over the past."[3] Blumhardt remained for Barth a man of the "future."[4]

Most of the church members in Safenwil were textile workers who lived in a very difficult economic situation. Here is a report about the conditions in the Aargau villages of Fahrwangen and Meisterschwanden where a wickerwork manufacturing industry was based. The situation in Safenwil was comparable to it.

The most important businesses — Gebrüder Fischer, Henry Schlatter and Hans Fischer & Company — became a topic of discussion in 1911 when the working conditions of their employees became widely known:

"The shortest shift was 11 hours. Workers had to work 12 hour shifts [in the factory] for years without any additional compensation — and they still had to take wickerwork home in order to clean it. Families had to spend another 1-3 hours at night for such work. And the 'wages': average pay for one hour was 22 Rappen! For 13-15 hours of work in the factory or at home, the princely sum of 4 Franken per day could be earned. But if a worker was 15 minutes late, she had to pay 55 Rappen which was more than the wages for two hours of work. The majority of the female workers 'earned' in 11 hours from 1.90 to 2.50 Franken."

When negotiation offers from the workers were rejected by the employers, a 31-week debate began. The textile workers union was asked for help. "A meeting took place on April 9. A union was founded and soon had 250 members."

The employers reacted with a "warning to all workers." . . . Those who had already joined the union were threatened with termination notices if by April 15 they did not leave the union. . . . The workers referred to the right of association granted in the constitution. Although the employers "took the advice of the government and withdrew the

2. Moltmann, *Anfänge*, p. 46.
3. Moltmann, *Anfänge*, p. 49.
4. For this reason the obituary has the title "Past and *Future*" (emphasis by Frank Jehle).

termination notices to all union members because they . . . were illegal," they later issued more termination notices so that "about 100 workers were excluded and the rest of the members of the organization expected notices any day.

"Finally, a major action was initiated: the owners [and managers] themselves approached the workers individually and presented them with written notices of resignation and tried to convince them to sign them." But of the 270 members of the association only 28 left. The meetings during the debate took place in a barn because workers did not have permission to meet on factory premises.[5]

Almost a year after his installation as pastor of the Safenwil congregation, on April 26, 1912, Barth wrote in a letter to the Basel theology professor Paul Wernle that he was amazed, after having been in Safenwil for only "half-of-a-year," to "find himself in among the socialists."[6] He also became the local president of the Blue Cross (an association with pietistic tendencies which fought against alcoholism and whose members had to promise to abstain from alcohol). During his time in Geneva, Barth said he saw himself in retrospect as having thought little about socialism or the Blue Cross (though, in view of his even earlier lecture in the Zofingia, this statement is somewhat of an exaggeration). In the same letter to Wernle, he says that "the pastor's best and so-to-speak only grist-for-the-grind" at that time had been a "well-thought out dogmatics."[7] Barth still considered theological work in Safenwil very important. Yet he had to get beyond simply "shrugging his shoulders over practical matters in question." He could not be politically neutral. In Safenwil he could no longer manage to float "above the clouds." He had to say yes or no "to capitalism as well as alcoholism." He could not simply watch these things from the window of his manse and present "a neutral 'Gospel.'"[8]

Barth did not become a member of the Social Democratic Party at first, though the five-member board of the Safenwiler Workers Union unanimously requested in the summer of 1913 that he "become a member of the association (and thereby also a member of the Social Demo-

---

5. Barth, *Kl. Arbeiten* 2, pp. 439f., with quotations from E. Marti, *50 Jahre schweizerische Textil-und Fabrikarbeiter-Organisation 1903-1953* (Zürich, 1954).

6. Barth, *Kl. Arbeiten* 2, p. 384.

7. Barth, *Kl. Arbeiten* 2, pp. 384f.

8. Barth, *Kl. Arbeiten* 2, p. 385.

cratic Party) and be their president as well." In a letter to a fellow student, Barth stated that "after considering it for four weeks, he finally declined the offer not as a matter of principle but for the time being." In his view there was no theological obstacle. Rather he felt "not quite ready for it, first of all, because he did not have the political knowledge and skill necessary for the job, and secondly, he was not sure how to integrate it with the task of ministry." He wanted "to do justice to both in a proper way." He was, therefore, "for the time being, for the sake of expediency, not fully a socialist," but it still certainly "could happen."[9]

Even though the young pastor of Safenwil took, from the beginning, the side of the workers of his congregation who were living in a difficult situation, he needed a longer process of fermentation and maturation before he could become a member of the Social Democratic Party as he did in the middle of the First World War. In a letter of February 5, 1915, he explained his — at that time, courageous — decision to his friend Eduard Thurneysen:

> I have now [as of January 26, 1915] become a member of the Social Democratic Party. Precisely because I am trying Sunday by Sunday to speak about last things, I could no longer allow myself to personally float in the clouds above the present evil world, rather it had to be demonstrated right now that faith in the Greatest does not exclude but rather includes work and suffering in a realm which is not yet complete. Hopefully, the socialists in my congregation will now, after my public criticism of the party, understand me correctly. And I myself also hope to avoid becoming unfaithful to the "essential" orientation as could have perhaps happened to me if I had taken this step two years ago. For the moment I have cancelled all party activity. My contribution consists in paying my fee and holding lectures.[10]

The text is an informative document: Barth is obviously not even at this point a thoroughgoing socialist. He knows himself to be obliged, as he states, to faith in the "Greatest," i.e., in God, for whom all earthly things have only a relative significance. He publicly criticizes the German Social Democrats because they voted in the summer of 1914 for war credit against basic party theory, viz., "Workers of the world,

9. Barth, *Kl. Arbeiten* 2, p. 574.
10. Barth-Thurneysen, p. 30.

unite!"[11] And yet he visibly wants to take a side because he does not think much of free-floating intellectualism.

Barth's closest friend, Eduard Thurneysen, respected Barth's decision, but for himself Thurneysen maintained a more reserved position. Although he too was a religious socialist, he did not become a member of the Social Democratic Party. In November of 1914 he wrote that his concern was "to work out the implications of a faith focused solely upon God which awaits his fulfillment alone," a "religious orientation determined solely from within."[12] Thurneysen wanted socialism internalized and deepened.[13] In a letter which has unfortunately been lost, he must have talked already in June of 1913 about the necessity of "depoliticizing" Christendom. Barth gave Thurneysen the following to think about:

> I do not quite understand what you presented to me regarding the "depoliticization." Are you saying that Christians should, in general, stay away from the life of a party, or merely ministers? Should we then leave the parties to those who are far from the Gospel? When I say no [with respect to the issue of joining the Social Democratic Party] I do so without a joyful heart, with a feeling that I am making a concession to wretched human weakness, my own and that of others. . . . But I cannot come up with this no on the basis of some sort of Christian pathos. I can only say: unfortunately, unfortunately — for the time being — I cannot do so.[14]

Barth was not the type of person who, in a critical situation, was especially reserved. This is why he became such a great force of opposition during the National Socialist threat.

After he was asked officially to assume the local presidency of the party, Barth began to work in the summer of 1913 with an intense theoretical devotion to economic and sociopolitical problems. "In the fall of 1913, he began to gather a collection of materials on 'the question of the worker.'" On December 15, 1913, he wrote that in view of such matters, theology was moved "seriously into the background." Barth feared that his "article on the personality of God," which was sup-

---

11. See below, pp. 36-37.
12. Barth-Thurneysen, p. 20.
13. Barth-Thurneysen, p. 23.
14. Barth-Thurneysen, p. 5.

posed to be published in the *Zeitschrift für Theologie und Kirche*, would be "for a long period of time, [his] final word of that kind." The article he was referring to is a large, systematic theological essay which he "divided into two parts"[15] and published in 1914 in this respected academic journal.

During that time a collection of materials developed "which consists of sixty-one, loose but tightly-written pages, 23 centimeters long, 18 centimeters wide. They were put together in a notebook of the same size." The largest part was written by Barth himself, but there are "occasionally entire newspaper articles glued in."[16] This bundle of papers demonstrates how intensively Barth worked in order to come to terms with the questions. He read works on economics, for instance, by the social reformer and Berlin professor Werner Sombart; Barth led evening readings of Sombart's book, *Socialism and Social Movement*, in the manse from mid-January to the end of March 1912.[17] However, despite his close attention to questions of national economics, he never seemed very familiar with the original texts of classic works on economics such as by Adam Smith, David Ricardo, and John Stuart Mill. Except for Sombart, the most important book he worked through was the 761-page volume *Die Arbeiterfrage (The Question of the Working Class People)* by Heinrich Herkner, professor of national economics at the Royal Technical University of Berlin.[18] In a letter to a friend from his youth, Barth regretted that as a student in Berlin he had missed the chance to "take classes in (political) economics." He now had to "pick up everything piecemeal." Barth subscribed to trade journals, e.g., the *Gewerkschaftliche Rundschau (Trade Union Review)*, the *Textilarbeiter (The Textile Worker)*, a paper of the consumers' trade union, and a newspaper for farmers. Daily he read the trade section of the *Basler Nachrichten* — "with much diligence" and yet "often without success." Many things for him were "still rather dark." His friends knew that he was not particularly gifted in mathematical and technical financial matters.

Above all, Barth clearly recognized that the education level of factory workers had to be raised. Besides his church activity in the narrower

15. Barth, *Kl. Arbeiten* 2, p. 498.
16. Barth, *Kl. Arbeiten* 2, p. 573.
17. Barth, *Kl. Arbeiten* 2, p. 381.
18. Barth, *Kl. Arbeiten* 2, p. 573.

sense (preaching, teaching, and providing pastoral care), he organized adult education courses in the evenings for men and women working in the factory where he discussed with them, as he described, ordinary, practical questions (work schedules, domestic finances, women at work, etc.). He wrote to Thurneysen that he did these things "without enthusiasm, simply because it is necessary."[19] Within this statement we see something which would later have even greater significance: though he was very politically active, Barth was at the same time against every ideological excess associated with political activity.

In the winter of 1911/12 he taught at the School of Home Economics, Health, and Bookkeeping.[20] The "formation of labor-union organizations among the workers" in Safenwil was "as much hindered by the factory owners as it was promoted by Barth."[21] Again and again it became clear how intensely the young minister identified with the people entrusted to his care. During the worldwide flu epidemic in the fall of 1918, he became the president of an eleven-member "emergency commission which had a budget of 6000 francs (a very considerable sum at that time)." And "now we are cooking soup as a matter of life and death in the school house for all who want it, and other helpful work with clothing, etc. shall follow."[22]

Which brings us to Barth's lecture "Jesus Christ and the Social Movement," which is a highly important document. He gave it on December 17, 1911, in Safenwil, only six months after he had been installed as pastor. The lecture shows how quickly Barth adjusted to the situation. It appeared in the *Freier Aargauer* in four parts. In response to it, the young pastor was severely and quite indiscriminately attacked in the newspaper by the son of one of the village factory owners. As a result of this debate, the Sunday morning worship service from then on was especially well attended. Here is a poignant example of the spectacular assault: "Reverend, you are still rather young. Therefore let me tell you as someone who is older that even in the twentieth century there is still a difference between theory and practice, and not even the oldest, and therefore no longer relevant, Bible verses can help bridge this difference."[23] It is

19. Barth, *Kl. Arbeiten* 2, pp. 576f.
20. Busch, *Lebenslauf*, p. 79; ET, p. 67 (revised).
21. Busch, *Lebenslauf*, p. 116; ET, pp. 70-71.
22. Barth-Thurneysen, p. 300.
23. Barth, *Kl. Arbeiten* 2, p. 410.

worth noting that the factory owner's son was only a few years older than Barth. Here are a few key passages from the sensational lecture: "What Jesus brings to us are not ideas, but a way of life. It is possible to have the most Christian ideas about God and the world, about man and his salvation, and yet, despite all this, still be a thoroughgoing pagan. And one can be a true follower and disciple of Christ and be an atheist, a materialist and Darwinist."[24] This passage is reminiscent of a statement made by Christoph Blumhardt, who preferred the atheistic leader of the German Social Democrats, August Bebel, who cared for humanity, more so than "some 'pious' people."[25]

Similar thoughts are found in Hermann Kutter's book of 1903, *They Must! An Open Word to Christian Society*. He wrote that the roles had been reversed: "The bold and mighty ones have become tired and the tired, lowly, and wretched ones have become bold and mighty. What the Church should do is being done by the Social Democrats. In places where God should dwell, he does not come near, and where people do not acknowledge him, there he dwells."[26]

Barth continued in his lecture: Jesus was a laborer, not a pastor. He felt that he was sent to the "poor and lowly." This is "one of the most certain things we meet in evangelical history."[27] On the social ladder one cannot climb any lower than Jesus. For him, no one was "too low or too bad." And this was actually "not an easy sort of compassion from above to below, rather it was the eruption of a volcano from below to above."[28]

Especially impressive was Barth's rejection of a one-sided, idealistic, and merely "inward" understanding of Christendom:

> [P]erhaps in no other area has Christianity fallen away as much from the spirit of its Lord and Master as it has precisely in its valuation of the relationship of spirit and matter, of inner and outer, of heaven and earth. It might well be said that for 1800 years the Christian Church

24. Barth, *Kl. Arbeiten* 2, p. 391.

25. Christoph Blumhardt, *Ansprachen, Predigten, Reden, Briefe 1865-1917* 1, ed. Johannes Harder (Neukirchen-Vluyn: Neukirchener, 1978), p. 20. This was from a morning devotion of October 25, 1899.

26. Hermann Kutter, *Sie müssen. Ein offenes Wort an die christliche Gesellschaft* (Berlin: Hermann Walther Verlagsbuchhandlung, 1904), pp. 34f.

27. Barth, *Kl. Arbeiten* 2, p. 392.

28. Barth, *Kl. Arbeiten* 2, pp. 393f.

has, with respect to social problems, pointed continually to the Spirit, to the inner life, to heaven itself. It preached, converted, comforted, but it did *not help.* [Granted], it has at all times commended help toward the alleviation of social needs as a good work of Christian love, but it never dared to say that the help itself was *the* good work. It never said: social needs *should not be,* and then, with *all* its strength, worked toward this *should not be. . . .* This is the great, mighty fall of the Christian Church, the falling away from Christ. . . .

The entire picture of the relationship of spirit and matter, of heaven and earth, is completely different when we come to Jesus. For Him, there are not these two worlds, but only the one reality of the Kingdom of God. The opposite of God is not the earth, not matter, not the outer, but evil, or as he would say in the powerful way of that time, the demons, the devils which live within man. Therefore salvation does not lie in separating spirit and matter in order that man might "enter heaven," rather salvation means that God's Kingdom *comes to us* in matter and on earth. The Word became flesh (John 1:14) and not the other way around! . . . God's Kingdom must rule over the outer, over real life.[29]

These are statements Barth remained loyal to for the rest of his life, even though certain concepts needed to be clarified and deepened theologically. In a "Bible study" in 1926 for the German Christian Students' Association of Münster, he said in an exegesis of Romans 12:1-2 where it speaks about the necessity of offering our "bodies" to God as a "living sacrifice":

It is decisive that the text speaks here about bodies. Not only the soul, the Spirit, the inner life! Here again, a hand is being laid upon us. It says: I need you, O man, completely, just the way you are. There is no better part in you. There is no such thing as the absolute contrast between spirit and nature, soul and body. That is not New Testament thinking. We must let the Apostle tell us: there is nothing more extraordinary in you. You are a sinner from head to toe. But God also wants to use you from head to toe. . . . We sin with soul and body, soul and body are reconciled, soul and body shall also be redeemed.

29. Barth, *Kl. Arbeiten* 2, pp. 395f.

There are no areas of which we can say: God has nothing to do here or this is none of God's business. It is not true that there is a religious sphere in which we are willing to listen and, at the same time, another sphere where life has its own laws, where we may not allow the light of God to enter in. But just as the whole is met by mercy, in the same way the whole is also put under the discipline of grace. God wants and needs nothing less than everything![30]

This is a perspective which is constitutive of Barth's entire life's work. The spiritual and the worldly may not be torn apart. There are no areas in which other "personal" laws are valid, but not the law of God. Similar statements are found in all phases of Barth's career. For him it was, at all times, an unshakable belief that Christian faith and our whole life — which includes our political life as well — are one. *The gracious God raises an absolute claim upon our whole life.*

For this reason it is worth mentioning already in this chapter Barth's foundational lecture, "Gospel and Law," which he wrote for a meeting in Barmen on October 7, 1935. Barth was already living in Basel at the time and traveled one last time to Germany, which was now under National Socialism, to give this lecture. The police, however, did not give him permission to deliver the lecture. Someone else had to read the manuscript while the author listened in silence. After the meeting Barth was escorted back to the Swiss border by the Gestapo. He would not set foot on German soil again for ten years.

In this lecture Barth emphasized that belief in the justification of the sinner means either "purification, sanctification, renewal" or it means "nothing at all," otherwise it would be "unbelief, heresy, superstition." The church must also, according to Barth, make "the *law* of God, his *commandments,* his *questions,* his *admonitions,* his *indictments* visible and concrete — *for the sake of the world as well as for State and society.*"[31] This is a theme that runs throughout Barth's entire life's work.

From his time in Safenwil throughout his *Römerbrief* period and from his lectures on ethics of 1928/29 to the early volumes of the *Church Dogmatics,* Barth liked to quote the familiar statement of the Swabian pietist Friedrich Christoph Oetinger: *"Corporeality is the end of*

---

30. Barth, *Pred. 1921-1935,* pp. 457f.
31. Barth, *Recht,* p. 89 (emphasis partly by Frank Jehle); ET, p. 79 (revised).

the ways of God."[32] This statement stands in opposition to a Christendom which is one-sidedly oriented toward a purely spiritual understanding of the hereafter and which rejects the body and therefore also the social dimension. In his early days Barth totally agreed with these words. Later he called it "a good even if exaggerated expression of a very necessary opposition to the flight of the Enlightenment spirit from nature, but it is not really suited for conversion into a dogma."[33] In 1940 he repeated the nuanced judgment: the "well-known statement of F. C. Oetinger that the end of the ways of God is corporeality reveals a historically understandable but essentially dubious exaggeration." It would be acceptable only "if one allows it to be read '*also* corporeality.'"[34]

While Barth continued to work out his theological position, certain basic impulses remained constant — among others, his strong interest in politics. The following chapter will show how several things changed, and mainly how they became more precise in his commentaries on the Epistle to the Romans.

32. Barth, *Kl. Arbeiten* 2, p. 398. Those responsible for the *Gesamtausgabe* make it clear that the sentence should actually say: "Corporeality is the end of the Work of God [. . .]," which Barth apparently was not aware of. He quoted from memory.

33. Barth, *KD* I/1:138; *CD* I/1:134.

34. Barth, *KD* II/1:300; *CD* II/1:268.

_____

CHAPTER 5

The Romans Commentary — Twice

A s an old man, Barth stated in an interview with regard to his time as a pastor in Safenwil, that then his "main interest in Socialism was the problem of the labor union movement." He "had studied it for years and also helped to establish in Safenwil (where there had been no such thing before) three labor unions which continued to flourish."[1] Such practical engagement was indispensable to Barth. In his early years, many things had not yet been sufficiently clarified theologically. It took *the disruption of the First World War* to force Barth to reflect upon his basic position in a more precise, *theological* way.

The outbreak of the world war meant for him a "double insanity."[2] *On the one hand*, the fact that almost all his German theological teachers agreed with the war policies of Kaiser Wilhelm II concerned him. Adolf von Harnack was present in an advisory capacity[3] when the emperor composed his call "To the German Nation!" on August 6, 1914. Its final sentences read: "We will fight to the last breath of man and beast. We will win this battle even if we must fight against a world of enemies. Never before has Germany been defeated when it was united. Forward

1. Barth, *Gespräche* 2, p. 550.
2. Barth-Rade, p. 33.
3. Agnes von Zahn-Harnack, *Adolf von Harnack*, 2nd ed. (Berlin: de Gruyter, 1951), p. 345.

with God who will be with us as he was with our fathers!"[4] Nationalistic concerns were here immediately linked with God.

The *other* side of Barth's "double insanity" had to do with the "capitulation of the German Social Democrats"[5] who, also in August of 1914, approved of the war credit requested by the Reichstag. From that moment on, socialism could not under any circumstances be interpreted as a "proleptic [anticipatory] appearance of the Kingdom of God."[6] Barth had to lay a more solid foundation for his theology.

The great milestone in his theological development is his commentary on the Epistle to the Romans of 1919. This large book (which became famous through its second, thoroughly revised edition of 1922) is one of several key works of the twentieth century. In the secular realm it can be compared with James Joyce's *Ulysses,* which was published in 1922. Of similar significance are philosophical works such as Ludwig Wittgenstein's *Tractatus logico-philosophicus* (1921) and Martin Heidegger's *Being and Time* (1927). Theological parallels to Barth's commentary are *The Idea of the Holy,* by Rudolf Otto (1917), and *Vom Geist der Liturgie (The Spirit of Liturgy),* by Romano Guardini (1918).

A brief note about the last two works: *The Idea of the Holy* is a key work in the history of twentieth-century theology because in it Otto reacts against a trivialized, bourgeois understanding of religion. God is the "wholly other,"[7] the *"Mysterium tremendum ac fascinans,"*[8] which means the mystery that simultaneously frightens and attracts. It is similar to Guardini's *The Spirit of Liturgy,* which is the Roman Catholic counterpart to Barth's *Epistle to the Romans.* This Roman Catholic thinker also reacts against an understanding of religion in which Christian faith and civil morality are confused with each other. The church is not here to guarantee the smooth operation of society and state. It is improper to ask about the "benefit" of the Christian faith. Going to church is not about satisfying personal religious needs. For Guardini liturgy does "not have a 'purpose.'" It is "not a means to be used to reach a certain effect," rather it is — "at least, to a certain degree — an end in itself. It is not a gateway to

---

4. *Kriegs-Almanach 1915* (Leipzig: Insel-Verlag, 1915), pp. 170f.

5. Barth-Rade, p. 97.

6. Barth-Rade, p. 33.

7. Rudolf Otto, *The Idea of the Holy,* trans. John W. Harvey, 4th ed. (London: Oxford University Press, 1926), pp. 25ff.

8. Otto, pp. 13ff. and 43ff.

an outer goal but a world of life resting in itself." "For this very reason, liturgy can have, strictly speaking, no 'purpose' at all because it is not there for the sake of man but for the sake of God."[9]

And now, with respect to Karl Barth. In both his Romans commentaries we find numerous repetitions of the phrase: God is "*der* ganz Andere," which stands in contrast to "*das* ganz Andere" in Otto (i.e., for Barth God is "*he* who is wholly Other" rather than "*that* which is wholly Other"), who in his holiness demands reverence and stands in contrast to the often-domesticated God of the nineteenth century. Revelation takes place "vertically from above." Our faith is merely a "bombshell crater," an "empty space." "God [is] the pure boundary and pure beginning of all that we are, have, and do; he stands in infinite qualitative distinction from men and from everything human, and is never identical with anything we name as God, or experience as God, or conceive or worship as God. God is the unconditional 'Halt!' to all human unrest and equally the unconditional 'Advance!' to all human rest."[10] Or, as Barth put it after the Second World War: God is "not to be understood as an expansion and enrichment of concepts and ideas which religious thought in general has usually had about God."[11] These decisive and deeply serious statements had a great impact upon the history of theology in the twentieth century.

At the same time, Barth spoke about his basic political position in his Romans commentaries, which is why it is important to notice the political ethics reflected in both books. In Paul's epistle to the Romans we find one of the few sections in the New Testament of an unmistakably political nature: Romans 13:1-7, which, in the King James Version reads: "Let every soul be subject unto the higher powers. For there is no power but of God: the powers that be are ordained of God. Whosoever therefore resisteth the power, resisteth the ordinance of God. . . . [The ruler] is the minister of God. . . ." This is a text which has often, especially in Lutheranism, and already with Luther himself, carried great weight. One can see in Luther's *Small Catechism* how the Wittenberg Reformer interpreted the fourth commandment, which for generations every Protestant

---

9. Romano Guardini, *Vom Geist der Liturgie,* 15th and 16th ed. (Freiburg im Breisgau: Herder, 1939), p. 58.

10. Barth, *Römerbrief* 2, p. 315 (p. 344).

11. Barth, *Grundriss,* p. 38; ET, pp. 35-36 (revised).

child in Germany had to memorize: "Thou shalt honor thy father and thy mother, that it may be well with thee, and thou mayest live long on the earth. What does this mean? We should fear and love God that we may not despise our parents *and masters,* nor provoke them to anger, but give them honor, *serve* and *obey* them, and hold them in love and esteem."[12] Luther thus spoke here — differently than the Bible itself — not only about parents but also about masters (which also implied political powers). The words "serve" and "obey" were also added by him.

It is well known that the conspirators of the unsuccessful assassination plot against Adolf Hitler on July 20, 1944, had to deal with the question: May someone who considers himself a Christian use force of arms against a tyrannical government? Influential Lutheran theologians in the first half of the twentieth century, on the basis of Romans 13 and Luther's catechism, went even further and had great reservations about, or were even against, not only *revolutionary* movements but *democracy* as a form of government.

In 1925, during the Weimar Republic, the distinguished Luther scholar Paul Althaus (1888-1966) — one of Barth's great opponents in the debate over National Socialism as well as over basic theological issues after the war — called democracy, as a form of government, a "disaster." One could not simply leave the social sphere to the "dynamic balance of classes and powers that are wrestling with each other"; i.e., the majority may *not* decide. "There needs to be a will responsible for the people as a whole which lies *beyond* the competition of interests and powers." Althaus spoke of the "ethical necessity of princely service for the people and of princely decision."[13] In his *Outline of Ethics* (1928), Althaus asserted that from a Christian perspective one should insist upon a government that "has the courage to exercise authority and power." The form of constitution should "make room for," rather than exclude or paralyze, *"a leadership [Führertum] which is free of majority will, responsible only to God, and capable of using authority."*[14] In the 1930s Althaus renounced Barth, saying he was actually demanding a "liberal

12. *Luther's Small Catechism* (St. Louis: Concordia, 1943), p. 64 (emphasis by Frank Jehle).

13. Paul Althaus, *Luthers Haltung im Bauernkrieg,* new edition (Darmstadt: Wissenschaftliche Buchgesellschaft, 1969), pp. 28f. (emphasis partly by Frank Jehle).

14. Paul Althaus, *Grundriss der Ethik* (Erlangen: Verlag Rudolf Merkel, 1931), p. 104 (emphasis by Frank Jehle).

constitutional state"[15] and, for this reason, did not fit in a Germany molded by Lutheranism.

Apparently Althaus was mourning the fall of the German monarchy in 1918. He could find no good words for the Weimar Republic, but after 1933 he did for Adolf Hitler! In 1934 he was a coauthor and cosigner of the so-called Ansbach Counsel, the manifesto of several Lutheran theologians who thanked God for the gift of the "Führer" (by whom they meant Hitler), whom they deemed a "pious and faithful sovereign." May God — as further stated in the manifesto — grant the German people "in the National Socialist system of government 'a good rule,' a rule with 'discipline and honor.'"[16]

But back to Barth and the passage in Paul: "Let every soul be subject unto the higher powers." It is instructive to see how Barth deals with this passage. He accepts it but gives it a new touch: not "Be subject unto the higher powers," but "As far as I am concerned, because there is no other way, *submit to the power of the governing authorities!*" (He thus translated it somewhat differently than the traditional Bible.) Barth had great reservations about the religious exaggeration of the importance of the political realm, or to put it in modern terms, its ideologization. He saw an exaggeration of the political realm in German nationalism at its terrible peak in the First World War, and in every nationalism. But another exaggeration of the political realm for him came in the form of a revolutionary attitude. (The Russian Revolution took place while he wrote his Romans commentary.) He had an especially allergic reaction whenever someone put a political judgment directly into theological terms in order to remove it from discussion. (From today's perspective, Barth was incorrect at the time in aiming his concerns particularly at Leonhard Ragaz, whom he attacked as an "attorney of the world-Judge" and as a man who had assumed the "mantle of a prophet."[17] Current research on Ragaz suggests that "the reproach uttered from time to time that Ragaz understood the Kingdom of God as an immanent power and that he identified it with Socialism" should be retracted.)[18]

Here are some statements which are characteristic of the second edi-

15. Busch, *Bogen,* p. 213.
16. Scholder, *Die Kirchen* 2, p. 210.
17. Barth, *Römerbrief* 1, p. 514 n. 65.
18. Dittmar Rostig, "Ragaz," in *Theologische Realenzyklopädie* 28 (Berlin and New York: de Gruyter, 1997), p. 108.

tion of the Romans commentary: Because the Christian knows about the "last" which is beyond the "next to the last" and therefore also that which lies beyond the political, he can become "concerned about the subject matter itself" *(sachlich).* He sheds "all pathos, all lack of restraint, and unbrokenness." According to Barth, a Christian is "no longer an angry god fighting with other gods. He becomes a realist." He is "liberated from that over-zealousness which is always a part of the Promethean argument against (or for!) the *status quo.*" Barth not only went against political conservatives but also against political revolutionaries. He also went against those who, in an *ideological* sense, were religious socialists. (Ragaz, therefore, could not be personally affected by this judgment.) Barth accused them *all* of maintaining their political position as absolute, and identifying and confusing their own standpoint with God's. Barth sought a "conversion from all romanticism to *realism (Sachlichkeit).*"[19] The words *sachlich* and *Sachlichkeit* are highly characteristic of the melody that plays throughout his political ethics.

In the first edition of his Romans commentary, Barth defines the "powerful state of the present . . . as evil in itself" and "as diametrically opposed to God's intentions."[20] He condemned "*all* politics" as "*fundamentally* dirty," as "a battle for power, as the demonic art of outvoting" (p. 502). Here Barth demonstrates that he was a reader of Jacob Burckhardt's book *Weltgeschichtliche Betrachtungen,* where the statement "power in itself is evil" occurs in several places (p. 501). Barth concluded from this insight that the Christian "had nothing to do with an authoritarian state" (p. 503), that a Christian could never "with all his heart, with real pathos, be a subject, citizen, or member of a nation or party" (p. 505). Barth advocated the thesis that the state had to be "starved religiously" (p. 508). Here is a typical passage (Barth puts these sentences into the mouth of the apostle Paul, who is the "I" speaking here):

> It goes without saying that you as Christians have nothing to do with monarchies, capitalism, militarism, patriotism and political liberalism. . . . Much closer to *you,* of course, is the other possibility of arbitrarily seizing in advance the coming revolution through Christ and thereby impeding it. And I warn *against* this! The matter of divine re-

19. Barth, *Römerbrief* 2, p. 471 (p. 513) (emphasis by Frank Jehle).
20. Barth, *Römerbrief* 1, p. 501. The parenthetical page references in the following text are to *Römerbrief* 1.

newal can, under no circumstances, be confused with human progress. *The divine may not be politicized and that which is human may not be
divinized,* not even in favor of democracy and social democracy.
(p. 509, emphasis by Frank Jehle)

Barth, therefore, clearly separates himself here from advocates of
Christianity who were sympathetic to the political left; a sympathy for the
political right by members of Christendom, in his view, was out of the
question. People who want to follow Jesus are often especially fascinated
with movements of social revolution because their goal is greater social
justice. For this reason — and this is Barth's interpretation of the apostle
Paul — Christians should "personally submit to the power of governing
authorities" (p. 507). Whoever rebels against the state as a revolutionary
thereby unintentionally concurs with and rejuvenates it. Instead of religiously starving it (this expression has already been quoted), one takes it
too seriously and thereby pays too great an honor to it. Barth aims for *politics that is free of ideology.* One should fulfill "one's duty as a citizen and
party member with a cool mind and without any illusions" (p. 513).

Barth would be misunderstood, however, if one were to hear in his
remarks a call to political abstinence. He was sometimes misunderstood
in this way, particularly in Germany during the 1920s, which mainly
had to do with the fact that in his new sphere of activity his past in Switzerland as the "red pastor of Safenwil" was not well known. For Barth
there was no basis for members of the Christian congregation to refuse
to work with the state in which they, after all, lived. It was in this sense
of political cooperation that he understood the verse, translated by him
somewhat differently than the traditional Bible: "Everyone should personally submit to the power of the governing authorities" (p. 500). As
he saw it, there is a "well understood and specifically qualified *duty* to
participate in the life of the state." He could not have made himself any
clearer. And yet he added that one must refuse the state "the pathos, the
gravity and the importance of the divine." One's heart should not be in
politics. The souls of the members of the Christian congregation are and
should remain "estranged from the ideals of the state" (p. 517).

In order to understand these statements, one has to remember the
euphoric mass parades which took place under Mussolini and Hitler, as
well as in Communist countries, where the "souls" of citizens were liter-
ally demanded by the state. But Barth continued and hereby returned to

the thought of a "well understood and specifically qualified" Christian "*duty* to participate in the life of the state": "[B]ut you may not deny [the state] your moral involvement. The state is actually, for lack of something better, the dutiful, 'ethical' order of life. . . . As long as the old man, the old humanity is still alive, you are also still under the law, and must also still orientate yourself ethically and therefore also still be political people" (p. 517).

> It obviously goes without saying that the political party system is not exactly part of that "which is true, which is noble, which is right, which is pure, which is lovely, which is praiseworthy" (Philippians 4:8) and that flamethrowers, mine dogs, gasmasks, aerial bombs and submarines are not necessarily tools of the heavenly kingdom. But precisely because we do *not* enter into a positive relationship with the state, precisely because it is for us — with all that is associated with it — the problematic creation of a fading world, for all these reasons, we cannot take all these strange things the state requires of *us* very seriously such that we might get into an argument with it *over* them. We fight it fundamentally — and radically — by *paying* taxes, *giving* the emperor what is his, *joining* the party, *fulfilling* the functions which are dutifully assigned to us within the framework of the not yet exploded political — and unfortunately also *church* political — reality. We acknowledge without hesitation or reservation that the state within its sphere has the *right* to make such demands upon us. (p. 519)

> We . . . still *have* political obligations. . . . We therefore accept [the "rulers"] without squeamishness and whining. . . . Giving them everything they can still demand of us on the basis of the general situation between God, man, and the world. . . . Fulfilling duties quietly and without any illusions, but *no* compromise of God! Paying the oblation, but *no* incense to Caesar! Civic initiative and civic obedience, but *no* combination of throne and altar, *no* Christian patriotism, *no* democratic crusades. Strike and general strike and street fights if necessary, but *no* religious justification and glorification of it! Military service as a soldier or officer, if necessary, but under *no* circumstances as a military chaplain! (pp. 520f.)

In connection with this last statement, it is necessary to read some of the horrible sermons by German and French military chaplains during the

First World War who were intent on justifying the war.[21] The Romans commentary continues as follows: "Social democracy but not religious socialism! The betrayal of the Gospel is not part of one's political duties. . . . And all such provisional agreements should not be made out of high regard for the 'rulers' and their case, but out of reverence for God, whose will we must follow and not proudly rush ahead of" (p. 521). A wide field of politics is opened up here — for a *nonideological politics, strictly oriented toward political issues themselves.* According to the second edition of the Romans commentary, politics *becomes a possibility* for members of the Christian community as well "where the essential competitive character of this matter is obvious," and from that "moment on where the tone of 'absoluteness' has vanished from both thesis and antithesis in order to make room for human possibilities which are perhaps moderately intended or perhaps radically intended." In this case "revolutionary over-zealousness" is replaced by "a calm consideration of 'justice' and 'injustice'" — calm "because *final* claims and accusations are here out of the question — but a cautious reckoning with 'reality' that has moved beyond the hubris of war between those who are good and those who are evil." As a moral philosopher, Barth stands for "an honest humanity and worldliness."[22]

Thus we are dealing with politics in which different parties are wrestling with each other in a substantive and fair way — knowing that there is never a perfect but at most only a second-best solution. *Politics is the art of "human possibilities," of that which is humanly possible,* the art of negotiating imperfect, but not imposed, solutions. As already explained in the introduction, because of these theological presuppositions, it was clear that Barth had to speak up for democracy as a form of government even if he did not idealize it. It was for this very reason that, from the late 1920s to the 1930s, he could have no sympathy for National Socialistic — or generally authoritarian — tendencies. From private correspondence we know that Barth was shocked over the "outburst of countless 'brutalities, childish nonsense, and stupidities we must now face daily no matter which party we belong to' [so Barth wrote in a letter on April 29, 1933]. 'Besides all that was happening to the German Jews' [as he

---

21. Karl Hammer, *Deutsche Kriegstheologie 1870-1918* (Munich: Kösel, 1971); *Christen, Krieg und Frieden* (Olten and Freiburg im Breisgau, 1972).

22. Barth, *Römerbrief 2,* p. 472 (pp. 514f.) (emphasis by F. Jehle).

wrote in a letter on April 21, 1933], he was also seeing before his very own eyes 'communists locked up' and 'Social Democrats suppressed.'" Those who wanted to "starve the state religiously" could not allow themselves to be beguiled by totalitarian ideology. When Adolf Hitler came to power, a theologian like Karl Barth *had to* resist.

CHAPTER 6

National Socialism in Germany

When Hitler became Reich's chancellor on January 30, 1933, Karl Barth was not able to initially recognize the full consequences of this radical change. Only two days after Hitler came to power, on February 1, Barth wrote to his mother that his family had come down with the flu. Hitler had come to power at the same time. But Barth did not believe "this signified the beginning of great news in any particular direction." Germany was "a body inwardly and outwardly much too heavy to be moved or changed through such movements." The new dictators had far too little personal stature. And the German people did not have enough of that "courage of life necessary in order to enforce a regime like Mussolini's or a counter-revolution."[1]

At this time Barth could not imagine that the Third Reich was the terrifying reality it showed itself to be with breathtaking speed. Basic rights were abolished only after a few weeks. But we would misunderstand this passage of Barth's letter if we were to read into it that he had even the slightest sympathy for Hitler. He simply underestimated his potential. From the beginning Barth saw through Hitler and his disastrous ideology. Already in 1925, long before Hitler's seizure of power, he took a clear stand "against 'fascist nationalism' and its 'anti-Semitism.'"[2] In 1928 it was said about Barth that he would form an alliance against

1. Scholder, *Die Kirchen* 1, p. 280.
2. Busch, *Bogen*, p. 34.

anti-Semitism "with anybody, 'even with the devil's grandmother.'"[3]
Hitler's obvious anti-Semitism made it particularly impossible for
Barth to sympathize, even for one moment, with National Socialism. In
his lectures on ethics, he had already stated in 1928 that there is "no
greater danger" for the modern state (he is speaking here with reference
to the democratic state) than mobilizing "one of the national traditions
— raised and united within the state — against others."[4] Barth did not
approve of a "master race" oppressing others, and least of all in the
heart of Europe.

Even though as a Swiss citizen he was in the first few months of
Hitler's regime outwardly somewhat reserved politically, he in any case
sent a copy of his pamphlet *Theological Existence Today!* to Hitler personally in the summer of 1933. With biting irony he wrote regarding the
mass nationalistic enthusiasm in which hundreds and thousands
walked through the streets of cities with flags and torches, that the
"chanting of the hours by the Benedictines in Maria Laach would go on
undoubtedly without break or interruption according to its order."[5] All
this probably deeply angered Hitler, if indeed he read it. In July 1934, a
year later, *Theological Existence Today!* was confiscated by the police.

From private correspondence we know that Barth was shocked over
the "outburst of 'brutalities, childish nonsense, and stupidities we must
now face daily no matter which party we belong to' [so Barth wrote in a
letter on April 29, 1933]. 'Besides all that was happening to the German
Jews [as he wrote in a letter on April 21, 1933], he was also seeing before
his very own eyes "communists locked-up" and "Social Democrats suppressed."'"[6]

It was mentioned earlier that Barth officially joined the Social Democratic Party of Switzerland in 1915, even if with a certain inner distance.
On May 1, 1931, he took the same step in Germany. Here as well he con-
sciously placed himself among the Social Democrats who were under attack from the extreme left as well as the extreme right. "He did not see
this step as 'an acceptance of the ideas and world-view of socialism' but
as 'a practical political decision,' by which he identified himself with the

3. Busch, *Bogen*, p. 35.
4. Barth, *Ethik I*, p. 326; ET, p. 192.
5. Fürst, *Scheidung*, p. 43.
6. Busch, *Bogen*, p. 37.

party which he now found to be most aware of the 'requirements of a healthy politics.'"[7]

In the spring of 1933, shortly after Hitler came to power, Barth was officially asked by the minister of education to withdraw his membership from the Social Democratic Party or else he could no longer remain a professor at the university. In a letter to his highest superior, he responded that "the demand to withdraw from the SPD as a requirement for carrying on his teaching responsibilities" was out of the question. He could expect nothing good to come either "for the church" or "for the German people" by "refraining from an open statement" of his party affiliation.[8]

Barth thus fought with an open visor. But in his capacity as a theologian he was active, first of all, within the realm of the church. And there was enough to do here because many theology professors and pastors did not resist the new regime but even welcomed it. In December of 1933 Barth stated that he did "not resist the National Socialist order of state and society, but resisted a theology that was seeking refuge in National Socialism."[9] We misunderstand this statement, however, if we read into it a certain political escapism. As a Swiss citizen living in Germany, Barth did not see himself called to step *directly* on to the political stage, neither did he have a realistic opportunity to do so. His life's work, which he passionately pursued, was within the *ecclesial-theological realm.*

In the face of National Socialism, different groups were formed within German Protestantism. Fortunately there were some, but unfortunately too few, theologians who, from the very beginning, clearly and publicly expressed their rejection of National Socialism. Here only the theologian and religious philosopher Paul Tillich shall be mentioned, who, like Barth, was a member of the Social Democratic Party. The forthrightness of his personality can be illustrated by an anecdote: In the early thirties Tillich was at a holiday resort and entered a restaurant "for a nightcap." Other guests who were a little tipsy asked him: "Professor, can you tell us whether there are any Christians in the world any more?" With a loud voice that could be heard all over the restaurant, Tillich answered: "No, not a single one. The only Christians in the world today are

---

7. Busch, *Lebenslauf,* p. 230; ET, p. 217.

8. Busch, *Bogen,* p. 39.

9. According to Günther von Norden, *Die Weltverantwortung der Christen neu begreifen. Karl Barth als homo politicus* (Gütersloh: Kaiser, 1997), p. 53.

Jews!"[10] Such a statement was dangerous in the face of the prevailing anti-Semitism of the time. Already in the spring of 1933 Tillich was terminated as a professor at the University of Frankfurt and had to immigrate to America. At that time in Germany, within one year, "313 full professors, 300 associate professors, and 322 *Privatdozenten* [adjunct lecturers] — a total of 1,684 scholars — were removed [for political or racial reasons] from German university circles."[11] Karl Ludwig Schmidt, a friend of Barth's and a member of the Social Democratic Party, also lost his teaching position in 1933 as professor of New Testament in Bonn and was forced to immigrate to Switzerland.

On the other end of the spectrum were the so-called German Christians and their sympathizers who welcomed National Socialism and were of the opinion that it could be brought together with evangelical faith. Since today there is an unambiguous assessment of this group, it need not be further discussed. Here is only one example: "Christ has come to us through Adolf Hitler," a member of the church council from Thüringen exclaimed during a rally of the "German Christians" on August 30, 1933, in Saalfeld.[12]

In connection to Barth, much more important than this is the *broad middle field* of theologians and churchmen. These (almost always men and very rarely women since at that time ordained ministry was not yet accessible to them)[13] were not National Socialists. Though with the best intentions, they personally wanted to differentiate themselves from certain aspects of National Socialism which were too vulgar and, at times, too brutal. They mainly fought against the state's infringement upon the Protestant church.

Particularly worth mentioning is the Pastors' Emergency League founded by Martin Niemöller. Whoever wanted to be a member of it had to sign the following pledge: "I pledge to execute my office as minis-

---

10. According to Wilhelm Pauck and Marion Pauck, *Paul Tillich: His Life and Thought* (New York: Harper and Row, 1976), p. 126.

11. Pauck and Pauck, p. 130.

12. Hans-Martin Thelemann and Hartmut Aschermann, *Horizonte des Glaubens*, 2nd ed. (Frankfurt am Main, Berlin, Bonn, and Munich: Diesterweg, 1968), p. 263.

13. For impressive exceptions see Susi Hausamann, Nicole Kuropka, and Heike Scherer, *Frauen in dunkler Zeit. Schicksal und Arbeit von Frauen in der Kirche zwischen 1933 und 1945, Aufsätze aus der Sozietät "Frauen im Kirchenkampf"* (Cologne: Rheinland-Verlag, 1996).

ter of the Word, being bound solely to the Holy Scriptures and the Confessions of the Reformation as the true exegesis of Holy Scripture. I pledge to protest, regardless of the cost, against every violation of this confessional stand. To the best of my ability, I hold myself responsible for those who are persecuted on account of this confessional stand. In making this pledge, I testify that the application of the Aryan paragraph within the Church of Christ has violated the confessional stand."[14] Whoever signed this pledge supported the cause of pastors with Jewish ancestors who were supposed to be (and eventually were) dismissed from office. The first twenty-two signatories in the first two weeks (from the end of September to early October) were followed by two thousand more pastors. By January 1934 the Pastors' Emergency League had gained more than seven thousand members. This was 37 percent of all active Protestant pastors in Germany.

But there was also an effort in these circles to recognize *positive elements* in National Socialism. The self-confidence of the German people, which was badly shaken by the First World War and the world's economic crisis, was being strengthened. Many people were suddenly willing to put their own personal interests aside for the sake of the common good. For instance, the theologian Heinrich Vogel, who signed the pledge cited above and later became an exceedingly "orthodox" Barthian, confessed in the fall of 1933 that the Creator was preserving the world through its orders of "race and folk." "Because God gives and preserves our life in our people, we therefore owe the people our life."[15] "Race and folk" were at that point still an "order of creation" for Vogel and were, for this reason, sacrosanct. As a German, one had to be ready to shed one's own blood for Germany, regardless of the political goals of the ruling government of any given time.

When Hitler gained a triumphant victory in the election of November 12, 1933, having announced a few days earlier the withdrawal of the German Reich from the League of Nations, leaders of the Pastors' Emergency League sent him the following telegram: "We greet our Führer in this decisive hour for folk and fatherland. We are grateful for the manly deed and the clear word spoken to protect Germany's honor. In the name of more than 2,500 Protestant pastors who are not members of

14. Schuster, *Quellenbuch*, p. 104.
15. Busch, *Reformationstag*, p. 13.

the faith-movement of German Christians, we vow faithful allegiance and prayerful thoughts."[16]

Niemöller, who was later sent to a concentration camp for seven years, also signed this telegram. In his sermons from 1933 to 1934, we find statements such as the following: Today, the Lord God "is taking our German nation down new paths." He is letting it "return to commitments which have been set for us and which we cannot shake off without dying in the process." Race and national traditions are counting "once again as real factors today"; they place "demands upon us," and "we cannot escape them."

> Yes, "praise God, all ye lands!" — "for around us" is emerging "the national awakening of folk and land" which bears witness to the fact "that we are still a young nation." . . . praise God, "we" Christians, "love our nation as our mother." And we have a "government which agrees with and protects the solidarity of Christendom and national tradition" which is our destiny and the "indispensable prerequisite" for the "outer rise and inner well-being" of the nation.[17]

In order to recognize the grotesque absurdity of such statements, it is necessary to note that the Third Reich "was a terrorist organization from the very first day of its existence."[18] A German study of the National Socialist seizure of power "counted [even] before the fall of 1933, 500 to 600 dead and around 100,000 short-term or long-term arrests. In Prussia alone, the number of those being taken into custody by police during the months of March and April [1933] 'was at least 25,000' not counting the 'irregular' arrests of the SA." Already in March of 1933, representatives of the National Socialist regime publicly announced the existence of concentration camp facilities. "Newspapers and even magazines reported," among other things, about Dachau.[19]

The supporting statements of the Pastors' Emergency League in general, and particularly those of Niemöller, are not quoted here in order to throw stones at these men from the comfortable position of one born later. Nevertheless, one has to be amazed at their blindness. Indeed, they

16. Busch, *Reformationstag*, p. 27.
17. Busch, *Bogen*, p. 73.
18. Scholder, *Die Kirchen* 1, p. 322.
19. Scholder, *Die Kirchen* 1, p. 801.

fought for those few pastors of "non-Aryan descent." But — and here we return to Barth — the Swiss professor of theology in Bonn had a very lonely stand with his insight that it was not enough merely to engage in ecclesial concerns.

It was very difficult and painful for Barth when his previous friend and fellow traveler Georg Merz (who was the first one in Germany to praise and underwrite Barth's first Romans commentary of 1919 and to publish the second edition in 1922 through a German publishing house) claimed that the National Socialist government was certainly justified, "out of national political considerations," in denying Jews the right "to assimilate into the indigenous population." As a Lutheran Christian, he could agree with this law. The state was thus defending itself "against the devastating effects of Enlightenment liberalism." "But because of the priesthood of all believers, in which the Jews were accepted 'through baptism,' the church was not allowed to exclude Jewish believers from church office — even though they should show restraint from it and in it because of the 'difficult situation they would bring upon the German nation.'"[20] Such a completely blurred compromise was intolerable for Barth. How could one disagree with the Aryan paragraph *inside* the church but show understanding for it *outside* the church? Why should "non-Aryan" pastors *within* the church have to be especially discreet and reserved for sake of the church's "ministry of outreach," even though they too were baptized children of God?

In a letter from September 1, 1933, Barth wrote that he, precisely with respect to the Jewish question, could "not take even the slightest step toward National Socialism." He also said that if ever the "call to stop were to be heard, if ever the border beyond which one could go further only in 'betrayal' of the Gospel were to be seen," this would be the place.[21]

On October 30, 1933, the eve of Reformation Day, he gave a lecture in Berlin: "Reformation as Decision." With utter precision he stated: "one could very well do something entirely different than believing," but there is no possibility "of believing and wishing still to be free in believing for not believing at another time."[22] "There is no other opportunity for negotiating again between the decision and the non-

20. Busch, *Bogen*, p. 108.
21. Busch, *Bogen*, p. 49.
22. Busch, *Reformationstag*, pp. 11 and 43.

decision."[23] With such statements Barth was aiming at the ambivalent attitude of, for example, the Pastors' Emergency League, who were *against* the Aryan paragraph within the church but *for* it within the realm of the state.

A few days later during a discussion with members of the Pastors' Emergency League, Barth stated the following (this quotation was the one later used against him more so than others during the trial that preceded his expulsion from Germany): "What happened this summer in Germany? Did it happen with justice or injustice? This kind of seizure of power? This removal of all other parties? This confiscation of property? What happened in the concentration camps? What happened to the Jews? Can Germany, can the German Church account for this host of suicides? Is the Church not guilty as well because she remained silent? I am just asking questions. Whoever has to proclaim the Word of God must say whatever God's Word says about such events."[24] Even if in interrogative form, Barth is listing here the National Socialist infringements and crimes, and he does so in an unvarnished manner. Barth was especially alarmed by the "the Jewish question," and not only about the fate of Jewish Christians but *all* Jews. On January 18, 1934, he wrote in a letter "that the present attempt in Germany to resolve the Jewish question" represented an obvious humanitarian, political, and Christian "impossibility." He was "not a prophet," but he "feared that one day those who were directly or indirectly responsible for these events" would have to suffer "an even more painful revenge than those who are now" suffering.[25] The "Protestant Church had to be ready with a loud No against everything having to do with the Aryan question, and also with an equally clear word of comfort and hope for its members . . . who were troubled by this matter."[26]

On February 23, 1934, he said to a rabbi that he "as a Christian could only think with shame and terror" about the horrors that were happening to the Jewish people today in Germany.[27] Synagogue and church, therefore, had to listen to the divine Word in a new way. He wrote to "one of his listeners who was troubled about her Jewish relatives": "[T]hrough faith in Christ who Himself was a Jew . . . , we cannot simply refrain from joining in the disdain and maltreatment of the Jews which is on today's

23. Busch, *Reformationstag,* p. 55.
24. Busch, *Reformationstag,* p. 106.
25. Busch, *Bogen,* p. 148.
26. Busch, *Bogen,* pp. 148f.
27. Busch, *Bogen,* p. 151.

agenda. It is certainly no coincidence that this attitude against the Jews is connected more and more clearly with a relapse into paganism. We certainly may not join in here, not even in our thoughts, nor out of thoughtlessness, nor out of fear of men, particularly those in power, and also not for some outward advantages or disadvantages. To repeat: we may not."[28] With this background it is obvious that Barth, with his uncompromising attitude, could no longer remain a professor of theology in Germany. It is not necessary here to speak in detail about all the unpleasant events that took place in this context.[29] The Pastors' Emergency League developed into the Confessing Church, i.e., a Protestant group "which since 1934, maintained an organized confessional presence within the Reich and among congregations over and against the dominant leadership of the German Christians." Besides the Roman Catholic Church, the Confessing Church was the "only major institution that eluded National Socialist liquidation. It, at least to some extent, resisted the totalitarian state."[30] But even Barth's "friends" in the Confessing Church thought him too difficult and not diplomatic enough.

This distancing of the Confessing Church from Barth was especially surprising because, of all people, it had been *Barth* who, in May 1934, by order of the Confessing Church, drafted the Theological Declaration of Barmen. Its famous theses helped many at the time to distinguish "right" from "wrong":

> We reject the false doctrine, as though the church could and would have to acknowledge as a source of its proclamation, apart from and besides this one Word of God, still other events and powers, figures and truths, as God's revelation.
>
> We reject the false doctrine, as though there were areas of our life in which we would not belong to Jesus Christ, but to other lords. . . .[31]

This is a recapitulation of the sentence from 1926: "There are no areas of which we can say: God has nothing to do here or this is none of God's business."[32] Barmen further states:

28. Busch, *Bogen*, p. 173.

29. For further detail on this matter, see Prolingheuer, *Der Fall*.

30. Wolf-Dieter Hauschild, "Bekennende Kirche," in *Religion in Geschichte und Gegenwart* 1, 4th ed. (Tübingen: J. C. B. Mohr, 1998), p. 1241.

31. Book of Confessions, p. 257.

32. See above, p. 34.

We reject the false doctrine, as though the church were permitted to abandon the form of its message and order to its own pleasure or to changes in prevailing ideological and political convictions. . . .

We reject the false doctrine, as though the State, over and beyond its special commission, should and could become the single totalitarian order of human life. . . .

With these sentences Barth was opposing totalitarianism generally and the installation of a "Reich's bishop" forced upon the Protestant church from the outside specifically. The Barmen Declaration stated that "the State has by divine appointment the task of providing for justice and peace and fulfills this task, according to the measure of human insight and human ability, by means of the threat and exercise of force."[33] What was demanded was a *constitutional state.*

In the beginning the Confessing Church welcomed Barth's theological support and was even enthusiastic about it. The 137 representatives of the eighteen districts of *Landeskirchen* eligible to vote, voted on May 31, 1934, unanimously *for* the "Theological Declaration." (Only one Lutheran representative went home before the vote, not because he disagreed with the content but because he had polity concerns regarding a declaration that had been signed *together* by Lutherans and Reformed pastors.) After the vote "the entire congregation spontaneously rose in the crowded church" and together sang the third verse of the hymn "Now Thank We All Our God": "All praise and thanks to God, The Father now be given, The Son, and Him who reigns with them in highest heaven. . . ."[34] But soon afterward August Marahrens, the bishop of the Lutheran Church of Hannover, who was the first chairman of the Confessing Church from 1934 to 1936, said Barth was the "greatest danger"[35] to the Protestant church because he picked too many specific battles with National Socialism. And even in 1953 (a long time after the war), another prominent representative of the Confessing Church, Bishop Theophil Wurm of Württemberg, spoke in disparaging terms in his memoirs about Barth and accused him of "totalitarian" thinking.[36]

Bishop Wurm should have shown greater reservation after the Sec-

33. Book of Confessions, pp. 257f.
34. Scholder, *Die Kirchen* 2, p. 189.
35. Busch, *Bogen*, p. 250.
36. Prolingheuer, *Der Fall*, p. 211.

ond World War in this regard! For even after "The Night of Broken Glass" *(Kristallnacht)* between November 9 and 10, 1938, "during apparently spontaneous demonstrations when 91 Jews were assassinated and almost all synagogues, as well as more than 7,000 stores owned by Jews within the German Reich, were destroyed or heavily damaged,"[37] Wurm wrote to the Reich's minister of justice, Gürtner, that "he could not specifically deny the right of the state to fight Judaism as a dangerous element." From his youth he had "considered the judgments of men like Heinrich von Treitschke [1834-96, historian] and Adolf Stoecker [1835-1909, Protestant chaplain at the court of the emperor in Berlin] on the subversive effect of Judaism in the religious, moral, literary, economic, and political fields as most appropriate."[38] Anti-Semitism was, long before 1933, an attitude in Germany (and other lands) that was deeply woven into the collective consciousness. Bishop Wurm had apparently been influenced in a lasting way by this dreadful tradition.

Back to Barth! Left alone by most of his friends, muted by the state's ban on his speech, and "retired" as a professor, Barth had to leave Germany in the summer of 1935. In his farewell letter of June 30, 1935, to his friend Hermann A. Hesse, a German Reformed theologian who was very close to him and who later suffered in a concentration camp, Barth emphasized that his thoughts "about the present system of government in Germany" had been negative from the beginning. At first he tried, "in spite of everything, to restrain" himself. But in the course of the events, his attitude of opposition became "so strong" that further existence in Germany "had become, so to speak, physically impossible." "With such thoughts," the Confessing Church could no longer "bear" him.[39] On July 8, 1935, Karl Barth moved with his family into a new apartment in his hometown, Basel, 186 St. Alban Circle.[40]

---

37. *Meyers Grosses Taschenlexikon* 12 (Mannheim, Leipzig, Vienna, and Zürich, 1995), p. 206.

38. According to Rita Thalmann and Jochen Klepper, *Ein Leben zwischen Idyllen und Katastrophen* (Munich: Kaiser, 1977), p. 209.

39. Busch, *Bogen*, p. 251. This is stated somewhat differently in Prolingheuer, *Der Fall*, p. 349.

40. Busch, *Lebenslauf*, p. 276; ET, p. 263 (revised).

CHAPTER 7

Back in Switzerland

In the summer of 1935 Karl Barth returned to Switzerland — involuntarily. At the center of his professional life throughout the following years was the *Church Dogmatics*, his massive theological masterwork which was actually never finished yet reached 8,953 pages (without indices) by the time of his death — a unique accomplishment in the history of theology![1] But Barth also remained politically active during this time. The Basel government appointed him leader of a "relief organization for German scholars." He not only made efforts with others to assist, accommodate, integrate, and further negotiate for mainly Jewish "immigrants," but also to finance the undertaking. It was in this regard that he corresponded with Bishop Bell of Chichester, Bishop Eidem of Uppsala, and Pastor Marc Boegner of Paris. All three were pioneers in the ecumenical movement. One of the refugees he supported was the Jewish pianist Rudolf Serkin, who, before moving to America, gave Barth's daughter piano lessons as a kind of "return favor."[2]

In support of this relief organization, a well-attended reading by Thomas Mann was organized in the cathedral of Basel. Mann read from his emerging novel, *Joseph and His Brothers*.[3] He valued Barth because of

---

1. According to Heinrich Stirnimann's counting; results in *Freiburger Zeitschrift für Philosophie und Theologie* 15, no. 1 (1965): 4.

2. Busch, *Bogen*, p. 269.

3. Busch, *Bogen*, p. 271.

his pamphlet of 1933, *Theological Existence Today!* He considered it "the first free and powerful German word of protest against the crime of Nazism in the western world." "What a courageous man!" "The only comfort in view of all this lying on one's belly is the work of the theologian Barth. . . . Only from this sphere and from this perspective, does a certain kind of resistance seem possible."[4]

Mann himself suffered bitterly because of National Socialism and because of the political compliance of many German intellectuals to Adolf Hitler. His essay "Richard Wagner's Suffering and Greatness" had been attacked in the spring of 1933 by a massive "radio and media campaign." Wagner had been embraced so uncritically by National Socialism that Mann's respectful but nuanced assessment of the composer on the occasion of the fiftieth anniversary of his death was considered an "insult." Important figures in the world of music such as, for example, conductor Hans Knappertsbusch of Munich and composers Hans Pfitzner and Richard Strauss signed a "Protest of Munich: The Wagner City." Given the circumstances of 1933, this text was a "perilous denouncement"[5] and made it impossible for Mann to continue life in his homeland. Coming from a secular background, Mann discovered in those years of suffering not only Barth, but also, quite unexpectedly, the power of the Bible. He called it the book "par excellence" (p. 202), the strangest as well as the most powerful "monument of world literature" (p. 200), a "comprehensive work of unpredictable spiritual power" (p. 202). He marveled at the magic of the Bible's sensual and spiritual character. The sensual character was spiritualized and the Spirit was sensualized (p. 205). It was only natural for Mann to participate in the charity drive at the Basel cathedral organized by Barth.

On January 5, 1938, the Swiss Relief Organization to help the Confessing Church in Germany was founded in Zürich through Barth's involvement. Barth invested much of his energy into this relief organization and held several lectures at the then famous Wipkinger Tagungen. He saw to it that his colleague Emil Brunner from Zürich was also invited to be on the leading committee of the relief organization in the middle of 1939.[6]

---

4. Busch, *Bogen*, pp. 90f.

5. Thomas Mann, *Nachträge* (Frankfurt am Main, 1990), p. 94. The parenthetical page references in this paragraph are from this work.

6. Busch, *Bogen*, p. 378.

Particularly during the war years, Barth not only provided basic support for refugees generally, he did so in concrete ways for specific individuals. On November 21, 1941, he made an appointment in Bern "to talk about specific cases among the refugees" with the highest official responsible for refugee matters in Switzerland, Dr. Heinrich Rothmund.[7] In connection with the persecution of the Hungarian Jews, he made contact on June 25, 1944, with Federal Councilor Nobs.

All over Europe Barth became known very early as an advocate of armed resistance against Hitler's regime. In 1938 it caused international furor when Barth expressed the opinion in a letter to his Czech colleague Josef L. Hromadka (at the time when the British prime minister, Chamberlain, was negotiating with Hitler over the destiny of Czechoslovakia and entered into the unfortunate Munich accord): "Every Czech soldier who . . . fights and suffers, will do it also for us — and I say this today without reservation: he will do it also for the Church of Jesus Christ which, under the conditions of Hitler and Mussolini, can only be destined to either ridicule or extermination. . . . Only one thing is sure: Whatever can be done from a human standpoint with respect to resistance, must be done today at the Czech borders."[8] Barth's former friends in the Confessing Church were horrified by this letter. Only shortly afterward, on October 24, 1938, he wrote a letter to Holland that the church, "for the sake of the Gospel, must want a just state and therefore a just peace."[9] "For the sake of a just peace, the church may not deny the state the right to bear the sword." If the state could "no longer protect peace in any other way," then it had to "do so by the sword."[10] Two days later, in a different letter to Holland, he said that whenever "political order and freedom" are threatened, this threat "would also affect the church in an indirect way." Therefore, when a "just state" would proceed to defend order and freedom, "the church would also indirectly participate in this defense."[11]

Barth was thus one of the most eloquent supporters of the armed resistance against Hitler's aggression. As a theologian, he even thought aloud about the *legitimacy of a violent insurrection within a country itself*

7. Busch, *Bogen*, p. 377.
8. Barth, *Schweizer Stimme*, pp. 58f.; and Rohrkämer, *Briefwechsel*, pp. 54f.
9. Barth, *Schweizer Stimme*, p. 63.
10. Barth, *Schweizer Stimme*, p. 64.
11. Barth, *Schweizer Stimme*, p. 67.

against an inhuman dictatorship. With a clear gaze toward Germany, he said in a guest lecture in Scotland in the spring of 1938 (when German troops were marching into Austria): "It could be that we are dealing with a government of liars and perjurers, murderers and arsonists, a government that wanted to put itself in God's place, bind consciences, oppress the church and make itself into the church of the Antichrist. It would then be clear that we can choose only to be disobedient to God in obedience to this government or obedient to God in disobedience to this government." Barth differentiated between "*positive* collaboration" with a state, and "*passive* resistance," "*active* resistance," and — as its strongest expression — "*violent* resistance." He raised the question as to whether Christians were allowed to participate in the "exercise of *force*" and pointed out that one is "here at the *border* of the church, within the realm of the *not yet* redeemed world. To live in this world and to be, at the same time, obedient to God" means, "directly or indirectly, participating in the exercise of force."[12] "Let us understand that we are participating in the exercise of force no matter what we do."

Violent resistance (as it took place in Germany six years later on July 20, 1944, in the failed attempt to assassinate Hitler) is, in fact, only an "*ultima ratio*," a last resort. But "fear of the *ultima ratio* of violent resistance" could and should not lead to the "exclusion of active resistance as such."[13] The world "is in need of men and it would be sad if Christians, of all people, did not want to be men."[14]

Barth got back at National Socialism in an especially pointed way during one of the Wipkingen conferences on December 5, 1938 (only a few weeks after *Kristallnacht*):

> . . . National Socialism is basically the anti-Christian, counter-church. Hitler and others who may be particularly responsible for National Socialist anti-Semitism, of course, have no idea what they have stirred up here. . . . Whenever this happens . . . : precisely the "physical extermination" of the people of Israel, precisely [the] burning of the synagogues and the Torah-scrolls, precisely the rejection of the "God of the Jews" and the "Bible of the Jews" — as the embodiment of all that should be a horror to the German people, with all these things and if

12. Barth, Gifford Lectures, p. 214; ET, pp. 230-31 (revised).
13. Barth, Gifford Lectures, p. 215.
14. Barth, Gifford Lectures, p. 216.

only the things that have taken place *already* — a decision is made: the Christian Church is attacked here at its root and an attempt is made to kill it off. . . . Whoever is, in principle, an enemy of Jews, is as such — even if he happens to appear as an angel of light — is, in principle, an enemy of Jesus Christ. Anti-Semitism is sin against the Holy Spirit. . . . And it is precisely in anti-Semitism that National Socialism lives and breathes.[15]

Barth therefore had to leave Germany. But in Switzerland as well, not everybody agreed with his openly polemical position. The people of Switzerland did not genuinely sympathize with Hitler and his regime. (It is generally known that there were some who did.) But many were of the opinion that one should at least not be allowed to provoke Hitler. Barth's clear statements seemed frightening and dangerous to them. An example of this is offered in a series of newspaper articles in the *Neue Zürcher Zeitung (NZZ)* in the spring of 1939.

In 1939 three daily editions of the *NZZ* were published, even two on Sundays! In the second Sunday edition of April 23, one month after German troops occupied Prague (making the Munich accord not worth the paper it was written on), there appeared an extensive lead article on the front page signed by a certain "Sdt," a freelance writer whose name was kept secret by the editorial staff. The commissioning of this article by the editorial staff raises concerns, as does the fact that Fred Luchsinger, in the wide-ranging Festschrift *Die Neue Zürcher Zeitung im Zeitalter des Zweiten Weltkrieges 1930-1955*,[16] assesses this controversy between Barth and "Sdt" neither positively nor negatively. Barth's relationship to the *NZZ* remained strained for decades. Only on Easter of 1967, one and a half years before Barth's death, did a kind of "reconciliation" take place: the most internationally acclaimed newspaper of German-speaking Switzerland invited the aged professor of Basel to write a holiday article on "The Mystery of the Easter Day."[17]

The title of the article was "Controversy around Karl Barth," and it judged the Basel theology professor sharply, and at points rather mali-

15. Barth, *Schweizer Stimme*, p. 90.

16. Fred Luchsinger, *Die Neue Zürcher Zeitung im Zeitalter des Zweiten Weltkrieges 1930-1955* (Zürich: Verlag Neue Zürches Zeitung, 1955).

17. Karl Barth, *Predigten 1954-1967*, ed. Hinrich Stoevesandt (Zürich: Theologischer Verlag Zürich, 1979), pp. 276ff.

ciously (and with little theological understanding). But "Sdt" did not deny that Barth had "undoubtedly rendered his country service by impressively presenting to many guileless and trusting people the unholy way of National Socialist doctrine and politics."[18] He also reminded readers that "Professor Barth" supported armed Czechoslovakian resistance and talked about his participation in the anti-Fascist newspaper *Schweizer Zeitung am Sonntag.* He mentioned the ban on Barth's books "by German censorship" and the "declaration of a ban by the Third Reich upon the theological faculty of Basel." But he did not show much gratitude for Barth's political courage and mocked that there was a certain kind of political "halo" around Barth. And he was particularly angry that "certain recent socialist" newspapers had repeatedly published critical statements "which Professor Karl Barth had made about National Socialist Germany."

"Sdt" was not a friend of the Third Reich. But he also harbored feelings of disdain, or even contempt, toward Swiss social democracy. Instead of "Social Democrats," he spoke pejoratively about the "Socialists." Concerning Barth himself, he did not like, first of all, that his "doctrine" infringed upon the "preservation of Swiss culture." Barth opposed the (popular and government-propagated) "home front" mentality and charged that the official politics of culture were "a dangerous result of neo-German strain of thought." And in an even more fundamental way, Barth protested against the view "that 'our type of state . . . is to be concerned only with the homefront.'" A further criticism was that Barth's doctrine would make the "policy of absolute neutrality" much more difficult.

"Sdt" was particularly offended that Barth challenged the people to ask God to make his grace "visible in the subduing and removing of National Socialism." "Sdt" was upset that "Professor Barth" referred to the Third Reich as the "new Turk" and made the claim that the Protestant church, as a "praying church," should declare its support for an "armed defence." The "thought of a crusade and the conversion of non-believers" heard in these words would be dangerous from the "standpoint of foreign political relations."

Barth was further accused of agreeing with Swiss democracy on the

18. All quotations in this part are taken from newspaper articles found in the private archives of the Old Testament professor Hans Wildberger (1910-86).

one hand, yet at the same time holding the position that the state "has no claim upon the soul of man and his capacity for faith" and is therefore obliged to grant churches "the right to freely proclaim the Gospel." The last criticism, of course, was on a different level and was concerned with the project of Barth's *Church Dogmatics:* whenever "Sdt" heard the word "dogmatics" or "confession," he suspected theological obstinacy and stubborn dogmatism. He apparently did not know that throughout his theological writings Barth distanced himself from the dangers of dogmatism. For example, in the first volume of the *Church Dogmatics* of 1932, we find the very seriously intended sentence, "the true results of dogmatics" are always "new questions."[19] In later years Barth wrote in the same sense: "In itself the Gospel is boundless, eternal, and therefore inexhaustible. No attempt of Christian doctrine can reproduce it in its fulness." Every human presentation can "only be imperfect, dependent on the standpoint of one's present knowledge." The gospel of Jesus Christ is not "a dead commodity" handed over to Christendom which one "has." "Beware of this capitalistic conception of Christianity . . . !" "The Gospel must ever and again be explored, sought, and inquired into."[20] The article of the *NZZ* makes it clear that the author was not really familiar with Barth's theological position. But here is the complete final passage of the article:

> Karl Barth has undoubtedly rendered his country service by impressively presenting to many guileless and trusting people the unholy way of National Socialist doctrine and politics. But the rendering of this service should not blind us to the *dangers* which are included in his *practical attitude* toward Switzerland. His doctrine infringes upon the preservation of Swiss culture according to the decisions of the Houses of Parliament. It hinders the policy of absolute neutrality to which the Federal Council has, in a solemn declaration, committed itself, the councils, and the people. It would allow the creative powers of public life to excessively reduce the position of the state. It could possibly even transform the secret opposition between the [two] confessions of faith into a loud religious war; at any rate, it serves to sow discord, insecurity and dissipation among Protestants. In their totality these effects could weaken the power of the confederation to resist.

19. Barth, *KD* I/1:284; *CD* I/1:268-69.
20. Barth, *Heidelb. Kat.*, pp. 12-13; ET, pp. 18-19 (revised).

To "Sdt's" credit, it should be added that Germany had repeatedly accused Switzerland of offending neutrality. The foreign political situation was delicate. It is remarkable that in the same edition, on April 23, 1939, the *NZZ* published the official answer of the Swiss Federal Council to a question posed by the German government. The Germans were trying to find out Bern's opinion with regard to a "message of peace" by President Roosevelt in connection with the German occupation of Prague. The confederation answered that it had "*no knowledge* of President Roosevelt's intention to make an appeal for peace to the German and Italian governments." The following passage was added: "The Federal Council trusts that the *neutrality* of the Swiss confederation, which is defended by *its own armed forces* and clearly acknowledged by Germany and the rest of its neighbouring countries, will be respected." A reading between the lines can discern a certain nervousness on the part of the Swiss government. There is *no* "knowledge" of the American initiative (which was reported through the media), and Switzerland's neutrality is emphasized. Under no circumstances should Germany or Italy be offended or irritated. The Federal Council does not dare admit that it agrees with the American president in his concerns for peace.

The *NZZ* was fair in granting the professor of Basel an opportunity to respond to this attack. (Under the seal of secrecy, the chief editor, Willy Bretscher, told Barth that the author was "Dr. Georg C. L. Schmidt, editor of the politically liberal journal, *Der Freisinnige*, in Wetzikon,"[21] a man who had emerged as an expert on primarily agricultural questions.)[22] Ten days later, on Wednesday, May 3, 1939, an article by Barth appeared, covering the entire front page of the evening edition, entitled "Necessary Dangers." It was a journalistic masterpiece. With polite irony Barth first of all "thanked" the *NZZ* for publishing the article that was written against him. He "gladly read" the article and "therefore also gladly shared [his] opinion." "What a re-

21. Letter from Willy Bretscher to Karl Barth on April 27, 1939, original in the Karl-Barth-Archive in Basel. I owe the reference to the Barth researcher Dr. Dieter Koch in Bremen. The corresponding statements in the first German edition of this book are hereby invalidated: the historian Max Silberschmidt was *not* the author of the article in the *NZZ*!

22. Schmidt's dissertation, "Der bäuerliche Aberglauben nach einer bernischen Handschrift des 18. Jahrhunderts," is kept in the state archives of the canton of Zürich.

freshment to be disputed with in such a way that one may hear it and then have the opportunity to respond to it!" In this sense he would, "for the time being, shake the hand of his accuser" whom he, incidentally, did not know.

Barth focused his response on the criticism that "his practical attitude" was *dangerous* for Switzerland. He distinguished between dangers that are to be avoided and those that are necessary. Evading a *necessary* danger will only give rise to an even greater danger. Concretely, and with respect to the criticisms made against him, this could mean: It would be an even greater danger if Switzerland would now, for her part, as an answer to the German blood-and-earth ideology, allow her cultural life to be one-sidedly dominated by nationalistic interests. And it would be disastrous if, rather than taking a realistic view of things, she would set up against Rosenberg's *Myth of the Twentieth Century* a myth of Swiss freedom. Barth wondered what would happen "if we also would now proclaim a kind of spiritual self-sufficiency on the basis of our national traditions that speak four languages," if we "also would now begin to toy on the side with anti-Semitism," if we "also would now confuse culture with protection of our homeland." In response to one of "Sdt's" statements, he raised the objection "that of the truly great supporters of the Swiss culture in the past," none of them ever "put national interest at the center of all their efforts." Barth asked whether it would be possible after all to preserve "this culture in such a way."

Barth had put his finger upon a very real danger in Swiss cultural and educational politics at that time, which from today's perspective is obvious: the tendency to isolate oneself and be nationally bound up within. Many authors who had immigrated to Switzerland had been banned from their profession. The Swiss Authors Guild said in a report in connection with the famous Austrian columnist Alfred Polgar, that it would make no sense to see official Switzerland support native cultural creativity and "at the same time allow the foreign competition" to enter the country.[23] As a result of the ban, Kurt Kläber, author of juvenile literature, for instance, had to publish his book *Die schwarzen Brüder* under the name of his wife, Lisa Tetzner, because legally she was better off in Switzerland. But with his most famous book, *Die rote Zora,* he succeeded

23. According to Werner Mittenzwei, *Exil in der Schweiz* (Leipzig: Insel Verlag, 1981), p. 124.

in tricking Swiss immigration officials in 1941 by publishing the book under the pseudonym "Kurt Held."[24]

But back to the *NZZ* controversy. "Sdt" had accused Barth of allowing "the creative powers of public life to excessively reduce the position of the state." He objected to Barth's postulation of a limitation of the state's authority on the basis of "the right, liberty, and responsibility of the individual Christian." Barth said everybody claimed that they wanted the Swiss state to be truly democratic, i.e., to be "built on the commonly shared responsibility of all its citizens" which, "according to its constitution and law," is "publicly accountable." But he asked whether such a state could come into being and survive as one of the most important "creative powers of public life," if it considered itself "absolute" or if it would "elevate itself to the absolute, to the totalitarian state." Is it not within its nature, is it not in fact required of the state to acknowledge its limitation? And by refusing to do so does it not endanger its own existence?"

And this brings us to the actual theological issue. As he did in other publications, Barth held that the free proclamation of the gospel would be the best guarantee for limiting the state and thereby as well its protection against absolutizing or even totalitarian tendencies:

> [W]e are talking about this radical opposite when we talk about the "free proclamation of the Gospel" or about the "freedom, right, and responsibility of the individual Christian" with respect to the limitation of the state. I also know [though] how often human failure has taken place in the proclamation of the Gospel as well, particularly with respect to politics (in both directions). Thus I know that it is "dangerous" to bring back the memory of this limitation. But can it be avoided? Tell me: from where do we think we can establish and maintain our state as just if not from there? Where else if not in this memory does anyone think we can meet the great need today of truly gathering Swiss Socialists, Swiss liberals, citizens, workers, and farmers, German-Swiss and French-speaking Swiss? Until then I ask permission to maintain that it would be even more dangerous for our state to be suspect of and suppress precisely this memory as one dangerous to the state.

Barth then claimed that the — totally abstractly defined — memory of God, the memory of this "wholly Other," the memory of him above

24. Mittenzwei, pp. 268ff.

whom, according to the famous statement of the medieval thinker Anselm of Canterbury, nothing greater can be thought[25] — that this memory is the foremost and primary task of church proclamation and, at the same time, would be the best guarantee that the state — even if it were a liberal constitutional state — would not set itself up as absolute. *In order to remain truly human, a state must expose itself to the danger that sometimes the church interferes with it in an uncomfortable way.*

The specific political emphasis of Swiss Protestantism, which Barth was aware of from its beginnings, goes back to the period of the Reformation. In the fundamental work *The Shepherd*, by Zürich Reformer Huldrych Zwingli (certainly not unknown to the editorial staff of the *NZZ*), one could read "that the shepherd [i.e., the pastor or theologian] should not tolerate everything the king, ruler, or superiors did," but had to "show each of them their error" as soon as he noticed that they were straying off the path.[26] The shepherd had to do what no one else would dare do: "Putting his finger on sore spots and restraining the bad, sparing none, standing before rulers, people, and spiritual leaders, to be impressed neither by size, influence, or number, nor any other means of terror, being immediately available when God [calls] and not quitting until they change."[27] Therefore one could not, especially in Zürich, claim that Barth's position was absolutely new or unprecedented.

Barth also later occasionally referred to the "good Swiss" Reformed tradition's understanding of the relationship of church and politics. In a letter on August 14, 1941, he wrote to Bern that "reference to life, and even also to political decisions, belongs to the heart of not only [his] but every proper theology in general." "Especially the Reformed Church in our country, founded upon the doctrine of Zwingli and Calvin, could, under no circumstances, deny the right and duty of making such references."[28] And even more pointedly, Barth wrote in a letter to Dr. Heinrich Rothmund on November 26, 1941: "The Church, dear Dr.! — I wish that I could also call this to the attention of your boss [von Steiger]!! —

25. Anselm of Canterbury, *St. Anselm's Proslogion*, chap. III, Latin-English edition, trans. M. J. Charlesworth (Notre Dame: University of Notre Dame Press, 1979), p. 119.

26. Huldrych Zwingli, *Schriften I* (Zürich: Theologischer Verlag Zürich, 1995), p. 271.

27. Zwingli, p. 278.

28. Busch, *Bogen*, p. 342.

is not after all a federal department which as such may or must submit or fit into the plan and instructions of the government."[29]

In the next part of his reply in the *NZZ*, Barth deals with the criticism that his position is dangerous for foreign politics because it provokes the German regime. He asks his critic, whose name he does not know, if, on the contrary, it is not necessary to tell the Swiss people "already now," that in a war that is possibly coming we would deal with an "irreconcilable" opposition, an opposition in which one could act "no other way." Barth had also previously said that we would possibly "have to send our sons and brothers to war and allow ourselves to be bombed." By speaking up for a just state, one had to face "death and — even worse, have to kill." Was this not necessary to say "in spite of facing the danger that our diplomacy is not so easy for us at present"? "The danger that we — when everything is at stake — because of all this neutrality, might not know *that* everything is at stake and therefore might fail — is an even greater danger." Therefore he would in all earnestness "stand up for choosing the lesser danger."

It is not necessary here to report on Barth's reply to the criticism of theological dogmatism. There were no new arguments in the response by "Sdt" which was published only a few days later on May 5, 1939. With the aid of a text by the "brilliant historian and State theorist" Alexis de Tocqueville, the debate culminated with "Sdt" once again urgently warning against "an intrusion of theology into political events."

Only a few months before the outbreak of the Second World War, a clearer position could hardly have been taken than the one taken by Karl Barth. He was a pioneer of a resistance without compromise against National Socialism within domestic as well as foreign politics. Wherever it had to do with Adolf Hitler, he neither could nor wanted to be neutral.

---

29. Busch, *Lebenslauf,* p. 327; ET, p. 314 (revised).

CHAPTER 8

A Ban on Political Speech

Without a declaration of war, Adolf Hitler attacked Poland on September 1, 1939. The Second World War began. Karl Barth was one among others in Switzerland who, from the beginning, stood without reservation for national military defense. Already in Germany, he early on supported a strong Swiss army. In December 1934 he remarked to a Swiss journalist who had asked for his position on the military, that "he was in favor of a stronger defence of the (Swiss) *northern border* to Germany."[1] When the war began, "Barth, almost 55 years old, volunteered for Swiss military service" in order to "visibly emphasize his call to resistance . . . although he had been discharged from military service since his youth because of health reasons." "He was sent with 'the armed emergency service' to a unit which, in case of an attack upon Switzerland, had the task of holding up the German army within the border areas for a while until the Swiss regular army could gather in the 'stronghold' of the Alpine fortress." The unit, as its members knew, would hardly have had a chance of survival. "The symbolic significance for Barth of his soldier's uniform" was also seen in the fact that he, in a letter to Bishop Bell of Chichester on June 19, 1942, "enclosed a picture of himself in the uniform with the remark: 'Resist the evil with *all* means.'"[2]

Barth was also personally acquainted with Henri Guisan, the com-

1. Prolingheuer, *Der Fall*, p. 178.
2. Busch, *Bogen*, pp. 347f.

mander in chief of the Swiss army who was also a "Zofinger." Unfortunately, there are no documents about the things these two men were discussing in August of 1942 on the occasion of a two-day gathering on the Rosengarten estate near Gerzensee which belonged to their mutual friend, Albert von Erlach.[3] When General Guisan was in a military parade, Barth stood next to him in his uniform, visible to all in order to demonstrate to the public his commitment to military preparedness.[4]

As mentioned in the introduction, the Swiss authorities took no pleasure in the Basel theology professor's will to resist. As of summer 1941, Barth was banned from speaking politically throughout Switzerland. His telephone was illegally tapped. Eduard von Steiger even considered whether the troublesome theology professor should or could be put in jail. This was due to the fact that the Berlin regime was deeply outraged, above all, by two of Barth's recent lectures, mainly the lecture "Our Church and Switzerland in the Present Time," given for the first time in November 1940 and then repeated in different places, e.g., on January 19, 1941, in the St. Magnus church in St. Gallen. In mid-June of 1941 the lecture, which had been published through the publishing house of the Protestant Society of St. Gallen, was confiscated by the police and banned by the censors. By these measures the government complied with a demand of the German authorities. In a sharp letter of protest, they had demanded "the confiscation of Barth's lecture" on April 9, 1941. The extent of the stir that Barth's lecture caused is also indirectly seen by the request of the Foreign Office in Berlin on April 9 "for further copies of Barth's lecture from its embassy in Bern. Immediately, [the Bern embassy's report on Barth] was sent to the headquarters of the NSDAP in Munich." Shortly afterward a secret conference of the canton police commissioners of Switzerland, under the chairmanship of Federal Councilor von Steiger, was discussing whether or not to take even stronger measures against Barth.[5] The Swiss ambassador in Berlin, Frölicher, "made great efforts" on July 12 to ask the government in Bern "to put a muzzle on Barth because of diplomatic concerns." Barth was accused of "disturbing a

---

3. Busch, *Bogen*, p. 355. See also Busch, *Lebenslauf*, p. 332; ET, pp. 318-19 (revised).

4. Busch, *Bogen*, p. 356.

5. Busch, *Bogen*, p. 339.

'proper' relationship to Germany," of "endangering Swiss neutrality," and of "possible charges of treason."[6]

Barth's lecture, "Our Church and Switzerland in the Present Time," was indeed very pointed. He said God was waiting "to meet a mass of men and women who would be sincere enough not to fall for the cunning, the fraud, and deceit of this time, and who would not enter into any contracts with the devil."[7] It is necessary "to make use of one's mouth to oppose foolish mouths." Those "who open their mouth the widest" are not always right (p. 169). Barth warned against "those who admitted that they were trying to conform, those who were trying to eliminate political opposition, to reject the necessity of Switzerland's defense, to directly or indirectly capitulate, and to virtually fall over to worship foreign gods. Publicly and without regard to whom, it should here be said that such actions are worse than stealing silver spoons" (p. 168). Switzerland is facing the danger "that the great steamroller of the so-called re-ordering of Europe [will] eventually, on one of its tours, also certainly reach this corner which, up til now, has still been spared" (p. 162).

The regime in Berlin was especially enraged over passages in which Barth vividly portrayed what a German foreign rule over Switzerland would mean practically. "A state-authority, not controlled by any side, would make it a daily moral principle to destroy or even to physically neutralize all those who resisted it. This would finally end in the systematic extermination of those who, because of their weakness, are useless for their purposes." It would be "unbearable if the church as well only [had] the choice of either dedicating itself to the cult of this state-authority that conducts itself as if it were divine or limiting its witness to an uncommitted whisper within the sphere of personal piety." All this could be "suffered in the case of an emergency, just as one has to suffer through epidemics and earthquakes." But one could not want it. "Having to participate in all this" is "unbearable because it is not right [but] disgraceful." Barth was thinking here mainly about "the rough and sly abuse of the Jews." This is the meaning and substance "of the foreign tyranny that is threatening today" (p. 161). "[T]he innermost center of this

---

6. Busch, *Bogen*, pp. 340f.

7. Barth, *Schweizer Stimme*, p. 170. Parenthetical page references in this and the next paragraph are to this work.

empire [consists] in the hatred and repudiation of the Jews. . . . But the Son of Man, who was the Son of God, was a Jew" (p. 175). There are many debates today about how much of the horrors of National Socialism could have been known at that time in Switzerland. Barth apparently knew at that point in time, in the fall of 1940, about the program of "euthanasia," the destruction of the so-called "life not worth living," as well as the persecution of the Jews, though it was not yet known to its most horrific extent.

Another lecture was also forbidden by the censors. On August 1, 1941, all of Switzerland was celebrating the 650th anniversary of the confederation agreement on the Rütli — a field overlooking Lake Lucerne where, according to legend, representatives of the first Swiss Confederation met to swear mutual fidelity. In this context the Young Church — at that time a very lively and active youth organization within German-Swiss Protestantism — organized three so-called country congregations who were meeting on July 6, 1941. Several thousand young people gathered in Frauenfeld, in Zürich, or in Gwatt on Lake Thun. "The warmth of the summer" did not keep the participants from "following the presentations of the speakers with close attentiveness. One could tell that many of these young people were aware that these were the most burning questions of the day and concerned every Swiss citizen and particularly every Christian in Switzerland."[8] The speaker in Frauenfeld was Georg Thürer, an historian teaching in St. Gallen; in Zürich it was Emil Brunner, professor of theology; and in Gwatt it was Karl Barth (he repeated the lecture a week later in French before an even greater crowd at Vaumarcus, located in the canton of Neuchâtel). The federal board of the Young Church published all three lectures in a booklet which was postdated August 1, 1941. Barth's lecture was additionally published as a special edition through the publishing house of the Protestant Society of St. Gallen (printed by Weber Press in Heiden), entitled "In the Name of God the Almighty, 1291-1941." The first edition of 12,000 copies sold immediately. Sixteen thousand copies of the second edition were printed. (On June 21, 1941, Hitler attacked Russia. Since there was no mention of it in the printed lectures, it can be assumed that the manuscript had already been completed three weeks before the actual meeting.) A personal copy of each was ad-

8. Karl Barth, Emil Brunner, and Georg Thürer, *Im Namen Gottes des Allmächtigen 1291-1941* (Zürich, 1941), p. 3.

dressed to the president of the Federal Council and to General Guisan. The choice of a small, little-known publishing house in St. Gallen is one reason the military censors noticed the publication just a few days "too late." And now the censors attacked: any copies left from the second edition were confiscated on July 18, 1941.

Emil Brunner's and Georg Thürer's lectures were *not* banned by the censors. The reason why becomes immediately clear when one compares them. The Zürich professor delivered a nice but rather abstract lecture about the idea of Swiss democracy. In the melodious dialect of his native canton of Glarus, Thürer called the young people with fiery words to the Christian faith and to love for the fatherland. Only Barth made use of the opportunity to take up some hot political irons. His lecture is one of the great political speeches of the twentieth century — comparable with those of Winston Churchill and John F. Kennedy. The following is about this lecture.

Barth began with the sober assessment that the Swiss are "a strange mix of people: Reformed, Catholics, idealists, and materialists of all kinds,"[9] which is why Switzerland, according to its essence, could not really be called a Christian state. Only God knows — as Barth says — what moved our great-grandfathers and grandfathers to begin the federal constitution with the phrase: *"In the name of God the Almighty."* But now these words are simply there as a sign. Next to them are other comparable signs, for example: Switzerland as a *"confederation."* An oath has made "the Swiss into a certain community as they entered into European history." And an oath "is an obligation that has been taken before God and in accountability to Him." Even "confessional and religious neutrality of our state institutions" cannot change this. Another noteworthy sign is the "Swiss cross":

> [It is] the white cross on the red background of the Swiss flag. Why was there not a lion or an eagle put on this flag? Why not at least the beloved bear, one who walks, like the one in Bern, or one who stands up like the one in Appenzell? Why not the bull of Uri who would have offered such a splendid symbol for the watch at the Gotthardt, for the "William Tell–myth," or for our strength and our occasional

9. Barth, *Schweizer Stimme*, p. 201. The parenthetical page references in the following text are to this work.

rage? Or why should it not represent our "cheese-making" or perhaps also a good many of our confederate cattle trades? And finally, why should such a marvelous symbol not represent our country's worship of the golden calf? . . . The Luzern Statesman, Philipp Anton von Segesser, actually suggested once to the radicals who were ruling during the seventies that they should appropriately substitute the cross on the Swiss flag with a sausage! But they were very careful not to do so. And obviously we can only confirm once again that this cross is simply there.

Barth's rhetorical brilliance is demonstrated particularly well by this passage. As the fourth and final sign, Barth named the strange sentence: *"Dominus providebit! The Lord will provide!"* which is printed on the rim of the Swiss five-franc coin.

It was already pointed out that for Barth Switzerland was not a "Christian" state. "The word 'Christian' says too much to claim that the alliance of the confederation has ever been a Christian alliance" (pp. 203ff.). The Swiss confederation was founded 650 years ago "with clearly *secular* purposes . . . and by the same *secular* means . . . it has been maintained, enlarged, defended, and transformed" (p. 206). And yet Barth thought the "alliance of the confederation, which in itself was not a church," was born and was preserved "on the *basis* and *foundation*, in the *atmosphere*, and within *reach* of the Church of Jesus Christ" (p. 207). Switzerland is, in fact, not a Christian state, but it is certainly "one that has been confronted by the Gospel of Jesus Christ, one that has been claimed by Him in an exemplary way" (p. 208). And this fact has inevitably very specific consequences: the gospel (which is actually a gospel of freedom) prompts the people addressed by it to order their political community not in an authoritarian but in a free way. In concrete terms this means: to order it as democratically as possible. By its existence Switzerland represents "the idea of a *community of free states of free citizens bound by justice.*" According to "its will of *independence* and *neutrality*" (p. 209), it seeks to maintain itself as such a community. "By standing up for itself, it also had to declare again and again that justice takes priority over power and that mutual responsibility which is freely lived out is not only better than the evil of tyranny but also better than the most well-intentioned tyranny" (p. 210). The political character of Switzerland is "comparable to the glowing of the Alps" — a *"reflection* of the

Gospel of Jesus Christ proclaimed to us and the entire western world, a confirmation of His resurrection from the dead, of the authority given to Him over everything that is in heaven and on earth, of His accomplished victory over all demons, and of the loving kindness of God who [wants] all people to be helped" (p. 211). These latter sentences reflect the rhetorical exuberance which could take hold of Barth, especially when he spoke about Christ.

Up to this point the military censors would have had no reason to take issue with the lecture. But in reading on, it becomes clear that Barth develops his speech in a way similar to the prophets of the Bible. He begins with a *captatio benevolentiae* — just as Amos did in his time when, in one of his speeches (Amos 1:3–2:16), he went first against the enemies of Israel before turning to Israel herself. Barth made the great turn in his speech in the following way:

> Switzerland could . . . lose its character as a community of free states unified by justice; it could cease . . . to be the memory of the old and the hope of the new order of Europe. It could become a corner of the world about which nothing more than this would be said: that there are all kinds of large and small people here who, more or less, earn their money, and who happen to have fun by making cheese, watches, embroidery, and machines as well as by being hoteliers and porters, mountain guides and ski instructors. . . . The inhabitants of our cantons are no longer free, they have become herds who, though they are diligently working and happily enjoying themselves, are, at the same time, irresponsible. (p. 212)

> The new European order — but what a different kind of new! — has come down upon us like a shroud. . . . (p. 213)

> [I]t would be difficult to emphasize enough when we speak of the 650 years of Switzerland's existence, that it has never before been in greater danger than it is today of losing its character and thereby its right to existence and consequently also the truth of those signs. (p. 214)

Barth saw the most serious problem and greatest danger for Switzerland not in the military threat but in the fear out of which it might accommodate too readily to the outer threat. Without even a single German soldier entering it, Switzerland might, as it rushes ahead in compliance, lose its individuality and thereby also its right to existence. To Barth Switzerland was at a crossroads: it would *either* resist the pressure upon its economic existence and accept the "prospect of seven lean years" as well as the "prospect of a military attack with all its typical consequences," *or* Switzerland would sacrifice its freedom and become "unfaithful" to the spirit and the letter of neutrality in exchange for "security," full employment, "bread and coal." Then it would not make any difference whether the German army would march into Switzerland or not. It would, in any case, have become "a cog in the machine of that order of war" and a part of the "new organizing of Europe" that Hitler's Germany had made its project (pp. 217f.).

Thus, for Barth, there was no doubt that material loss with freedom was preferred to a good life with a loss of this freedom. In the following passages of his speech, he became even more concrete. He put his finger on various wounds of the domestic and foreign politics of the time. Barth charged that at present in the confederation not everyone was doing equally well, but the "economically weak ones," the "bulk of the population" (p. 219), in particular, were doing poorly. In addition, he criticized the fact that the Social Democratic Party, "as the strongest political representative of the Swiss workers, and at the same time the largest of all political parties" (p. 220), was not represented in the coalition that was in power in Bern. What was more important to Switzerland: "the favor or disfavor of foreign countries" or the unity of the Swiss people "in relation to foreign countries"? Regarding the much-discussed question at the time of whether seven or nine representatives in the Federal Council would be preferable, Barth thought it was not very important. What was important was the actual "life-question," namely, whether "the voice of those less well-off" could be heard in places where, "with great authority," the future of Switzerland was decided (p. 221). It is important to note that this was said during the time of an authoritarian regime when some of the democratic rules of the game had been suspended. The Federal Council during the war years was equipped with greater power than the written constitution had intended. It took more than two years before Barth's demand (and, of course, the demand of others too) of Social Democratic representation within the government was fulfilled, when the two Houses of Parliament on December 15, 1943, elected Ernst Nobs to serve in the Federal Council.

Barth found further fault in the restriction of freedom of press and speech. He rightly mentioned that products of the Swiss press were already forbidden in Germany. If then, because of German pressure, certain things were being withheld at home as well, this would be an improper accommodation to Germany. Especially offensive was the present secrecy of the censors toward the population. "Swiss neutrality, as one of a free alliance of free states, [stands and falls] by having a *public* mind which can be newly formed again and again by an *open* consideration of the facts and by an *open* discussion by the Swiss themselves. . . . What then is the purpose of covering up, more and more eagerly, the mouths and ears of the Swiss people?" (p. 223). We are dealing here with an important aspect of Barth's political ethics. In his view democracy works only when free public discourse can occur and when everyone is informed as much as possible about the pending business of the state. Politics behind closed doors and a democracy worthy of its name will not go together.

Barth then criticized the foreign politics of the time. Germans entering the country with official travel documents were received most politely of all — even though they might be National Socialists — whereas refugees without papers were often not even allowed to come in. Immigrants were also treated shamefully. In the seventeenth and nineteenth centuries there had been a "generous and far-sighted immigration policy." The things done today in this regard, "even given an understanding of all the present difficulties," could neither be called generous nor far-sighted.

In his fifth and final point, Barth criticized the extent to which Switzerland had accommodated the Third Reich in political-economic matters, though he did not deny that certain concessions were inevitable. With the export of agricultural and industrial products, Switzerland was relieving "the labor market of the Axis countries in the sense that every hand [in Switzerland] participating in these exports, was freeing a hand on the outside . . . for work in the war-economy." Switzerland therefore "was, in a foolish way indirectly, serving in the war against England." With utter directness Barth asked whether any good could come from "secretly preventing the Swiss people from knowing at least what the foreign trade statistics were." Was there no other way "but for Switzerland to provide foreign countries . . . with complete or half-complete war materials"?

It must have been particularly offensive to officials in Bern that Barth openly publicized the fact that the confederation had advanced the German Reich between 800 million and 1 billion Swiss francs and made itself thereby "the financial backer of the Axis power and in this respect also an accomplice in the war." The question whether Switzerland will ever get the money back is not as important. Much more important is "the question whether it is good and beneficial." By this way, "obviously, the independent state will gradually, in all quietness, become a dependent state" (pp. 225f.).

All in all, this lecture showed how amazingly clear-sighted Barth was — not only theologically but also politically. Here are two more detailed examples of political remarks made by Barth from the same period of his life. On the national day of prayer in September of 1942, Barth published an eight-page pamphlet in St. Gallen which contained the following words:

> [The heritage of our country] has developed a leak . . . which will not be fixed for a long time, if at all. We came up with the official untruth, which we made our own, that the battle for justice or injustice that is moving the world today . . . does not concern us inwardly either. We have a new attitude in Switzerland, selfishly focused upon its own preservation . . . we have invented and put into effect a new right of (political) asylum which is of little comfort and help to those who were once free and are now persecuted.[10]

With respect to the collection for the refugee relief organizations that began a month later on October 22, 1942, Barth wrote:

> The refugees are our concern: not because they are good and valuable people, but because they are today the lowest, the most wretched people in the whole world and as such they knock on our doors, [and because their] inseparable companion is the Saviour. They are our concern: not although they are Jews, but precisely because they are Jews and as such are the Saviour's physical brothers. . . . The refugees (whether they know it or not) are honoring us by seeing our land as a last refuge of justice and mercy, and by coming to it. . . . We see in the refugees that which we have been miraculously spared of. It is cer-

10. Busch, *Bogen*, p. 356.

tainly true that today we are not doing all that well either. But again, it is also true that we are at least taken pretty good care of, and are taken such good care of that we are rich in comparison to these unhappy people. Can we bear this without wanting to help them with all our might?[11]

This was at a time when the Swiss border was completely sealed off from Jewish refugees. As we read these sentences today, it is regrettable that the Swiss officials in those critical years were not a bit more willing to listen to the "Swiss voice" of the difficult theologian.

In a letter shortly before the end of the Second World War, Barth said that, as a Swiss citizen, he "had been responsible for and somehow had to share in the consequences" of all those things the Federal Council had done in presenting "the Swiss face to the world in these years."[12] Or in an even sharper statement made in an interview in the newspaper *Die Weltwoche* at Christmas 1946: the Rhine River would not "wash away" the fact that Switzerland "rejected almost 100,000 refugees." The "treatment of those taken in" had been "shameful."[13]

11. Busch, *Bogen*, p. 358.
12. Barth, *Offene Briefe*, p. 17. See above, p. 1.
13. Reprint in *Weltwoche* (December 24, 1997), p. 16.

CHAPTER 9

For a New Friendship with Germany

"*A silent community, merely observing the events of the time, would not be a Christian community.*"[1] This quotation from Barth would be a suitable motto for all chapters of this book. On this basis Barth, as a Christian theologian and counselor, made it his business to engage, ever anew, in so-called worldly matters — as a pastor in Safenwil in the situation of the textile workers, as a professor in Bonn in the debates regarding National Socialism, and after his return to Switzerland with respect to the way the Swiss were dealing with the threat of National Socialism. The sentence is from a lecture Barth delivered on July 23, 1944, at an Oberaargau district celebration in the church of Dürrenroth, entitled "Promise and Responsibility of the Christian Congregation in Today's Events." Since his troublesome lecture on official Switzerland, "In the Name of God the Almighty," on July 6, 1941, Barth had not given any political lectures, having been banned from speaking. (Only on British radio could his political speeches still be heard — to the annoyance of Swiss officials.) During his visit to the St. Magnus church of St. Gallen on January 4, 1943, he spoke in a very "tame," theological way on the theme "Fellowship in the Church."[2] But on January 31, 1943, the German troops capitulated near Stalingrad. The war took a turn in favor of

---

1. Barth, *Schweizer Stimme*, p. 324.
2. Hans Martin Stückelberger, *50 Jahre Freie protestantische Vereinigung St. Gallen, 1919-1969* (St. Gallen, n.d.), pp. 98f.

the Allies. The invasion of Normandy began on June 6, 1944. Barth was allowed to speak again.

In his lecture on July 23, 1944, Barth said God did not "give us time and did not let us participate in the events of the day in order that we would act as if all this were none of our concern." Whoever here refuses "to look upon humanity — as if he himself were not also human! — would certainly miss the divine as well."[3] Because God became man in Jesus Christ, according to the Christian confession of faith, the divine and the human were inseparable for Barth. "Better that [the Christian congregation] stand up for the weak three times too often than one time too less, better to raise its voice unpleasantly loud where justice and freedom are endangered than to be pleasantly silent!"[4] Perhaps Barth himself wrote the best commentary on these programmatic sentences from his Dürrenroth lecture in 1955, when he noted in his *Church Dogmatics* that "conversion and renewal" is not an "end in itself," as it often has been misunderstood by "an all too egocentric Christendom." It is not enough that an individual converts only "for his own sake and for himself" and not "to God the Lord." Conversion is necessary for entering into the "service" of God's work here on earth and for being a "witness" to God's work with respect to the entire "cosmos."[5] As one's being is converted and renewed, "one has to also accept, together in and with his own personal responsibility, his public responsibility."[6] This is a theme found throughout Barth's entire life's work.

Toward the end of the war Barth turned to a question that was new at the time. The defeat of Germany and the end of National Socialism was only a matter of time. The relationship to Germany therefore became a central theme. It seemed then to be crystal clear to almost everyone in Switzerland that National Socialist Germany, or even Germany in general, would be rejected or condemned. Barth himself recounts the following episode from that time:

It happened in Basel that among and besides the hospitably received stream of Alsatian refugees, there was also a detached unit of German soldiers who crossed our border. An SS officer had tried to keep them

3. Barth, *Schweizer Stimme*, pp. 311f.
4. Barth, *Schweizer Stimme*, p. 329.
5. Barth, *KD* IV/2:639; *CD* IV/2:565 (revised).
6. Barth, *KD* IV/2:640.

from doing so. They had shot him down. Apparently they were not only tired of the war, but tired of Hitler as well. But they were still wearing the German uniform. These very same people then were in one of our suburbs being scolded as wearers of this uniform, being insulted and spit upon by the Swiss audience — apparently especially by the women.[7]

Barth, who, at the end of the thirties and the beginning of the forties, had tirelessly called for resistance — even for armed resistance — against Germany, now interceded politically in a new direction: *even the German people now lying on the ground deserve to be treated humanely* and not with utter vindictiveness. In his lecture in Dürrenroth, Barth said that Jesus Christ, "the reconciliation of our sins," was also meant for Germans, *"even for that unhappy man in whose name all the horrors of these years have been summed up."*[8] Barth meant by this Adolf Hitler, against whom, three days earlier on July 20, 1944, an unsuccessful assassination attempt had been made.

Especially informative is Barth's important lecture "The Germans and Us," which he delivered in French and German in January and February of 1945 in Couvet, Neuchâtel, Schönenwerd, Rohrbach, Olten, Arlesheim, Aarau, Geneva, Le Locle, La Chaux-de-Fonds, Bern, Glarus, and finally St. Gallen.[9] In St. Gallen the huge St. Lawrence church was overcrowded.[10] Though the lecture was unusually long, the people listened to it breathlessly. The numerous places in which Barth spoke demonstrates, on the one hand, how important this lecture was to *him,* and on the other hand, how intensely sympathetic the *public* was toward his, at the time, probably for many, unusual train of thought. In this lecture Barth tried to describe the situation of a Germany lying flat on the ground, and asserted the thesis: *The German people now especially need the friendship of their neighbor.* There "cannot be an anger ever so righteous that we may now truly let the sun go down on it."[11] We have no idea "where the German worker, the German farmer, the German pastor, the

7. Barth, *Schweizer Stimme,* p. 334.
8. Barth, *Schweizer Stimme,* p. 331.
9. According to Busch, *Lebenslauf,* p. 337; ET, p. 323 (revised).
10. I owe this information to the late Prof. Dr. Georg Thürer, Teufen.
11. Barth, *Schweizer Stimme,* p. 337. The page references in the following text are to this work.

German woman actually stand and where they are to be sought" (p. 338). What the Germans need are "friends" (p. 350). And Swiss men and women owe them a new friendship (pp. 350f.). Yet Barth did not deny that, in the context of the German people's fate, the word "guilt" also had to have a use (p. 353). He did not want to face them in a soft, sentimental way. "It is also known that in a sincere friendship" there are times when disagreements occur, and at that time the other, "with utmost certainty," needs the disagreement "for his own sake" (p. 357).

Particularly central, and in a certain way also spectacular, were the following sentences which Barth stylized in the form of Matthew 11:28ff. as *the speech of Christ addressed to the Germans:*

> Come unto Me, all you unpleasant ones, you bad Hitler boys and girls, you brutal SS soldiers, you wicked Gestapo scoundrels, you sad compromisers and collaborators, all you herds of people who have patiently and stupidly followed your so-called Führer! Come unto Me, you guilty ones and you accomplices, who now receive and have to receive what your deeds are worth! Come unto Me, I know you well but I do not ask who you are and what you have done. I only see that you are at the end of your rope and must start all over again whether you like it or not. I want to refresh you and precisely with you, I now want to start anew from the very bottom! . . . I am for you! I am your friend! (pp. 354f.)

This is a challenging combination of unvarnished declaration of German failure on the one hand, and on the other an extravagant offer of a new, religiously grounded, beginning on the basis of free grace.

In the second part of this important lecture, Barth spoke very insistently about the *Swiss* failure during the Second World War: "The Official Face of Switzerland" (and regrettably, this is the one that really matters) "during these years was certainly a very smug one, but," unfortunately, it was all in all a "much too smug one." Swiss men and women "behaved and proved themselves in those years only as Swiss and not as good Europeans." And precisely for that reason they "neither did behave and prove themselves in these years to be truly good Swiss either" (p. 368).[12] "[T]he prayer: May God have mercy on the Germans! [would] be most inappropriate . . . , if it were not well grounded in the most sincere *Miserere nobis!*

12. See above, p. 1.

[Have mercy on us!]. And therefore it would mean, broadly, that God might have mercy on us *all*" (p. 369). What is so extraordinary about this speech is that it does not mince words with respect to Germany at all. At one point, in unsurpassed sharpness, it says that not only a solidarity but even an *identity of National Socialism and "inhumanity"* had to be postulated (pp. 337f.). And yet Barth never adopted a condescending, pedantic attitude toward Germany. He truly tried to speak as a friend, and as one who was also aware of the weaknesses and failures of Switzerland and its men and women.

Briefly, though it should actually go without saying: Barth's lecture "The Germans and Us" was taken note of in Germany *after* the war. And there many, though not all, refused to take hold of the hand Barth extended them — or did so only halfway. Barth received letters which accused him of criticizing the German people too severely. As a particularly irritating example we shall quote sentences from 1958 by the renowned scholar, German professor of Old Testament, Friedrich Baumgärtel:

> [W]ho is Karl Barth that he is attacking us Germans in face of our collapse. . . . Would . . . that he had been silent before he pedantically . . . spoke into a world which was totally unfamiliar to him . . . , who never in his life endured the horror of battle and the unspeakable fatigue of a soldier, who never had to do military service for years on end in an army robbed of its leadership, of all military and human dignity, in a depressing conflict of heart that paralyzes every human joy, who never in his life, not even for one hour, had to be in a basement, trembling under the impact of bombs and filled with dust choking your breath, who never in his life had to do without sufficient sleep for nights and weeks on end, who was never hungry or cold, who never had his own children in the Hitler Youth, in the labor force, or on the field — would that he had first quietly, and for a long time, listened in this world which is totally unfamiliar to him, in order to catch at least a glimpse of the German man of that time! . . . Who is Karl Barth that he attacked us Germans early in 1945![13]

A similar situation arose with Bishop Theophil Wurm,[14] who accused Barth in his memoirs of "totalitarian" thinking. With respect to

13. Prolingheuer, *Der Fall*, p. 209.
14. See above, pp. 54-55.

Barth's role in 1934, he said it had been his own concern to find a "peaceful relationship to the [Hitler-] state"; "but in light of Barth's thoughts," it was unfortunately not possible to grant "tolerance in the Church in the liberal sense." The intellectual "affinity" of Barth's theology "with the totalitarian state" was too great. Particularly because Barth's "thinking was also totalitarian," he was not able to agree "to a middle course,"[15] as if, in Wurm's view, it were actually possible to agree on an acceptable compromise between the Christian faith and National Socialism that despises man!

Another example of German "ingratitude" is the German journalist Heinz Zahrnt's best-seller *The Question of God*, which, to this day, is widely influencing public opinion about Barth in Germany. Zahrnt stated that "Barth's diverse comments about relevant political questions were always used, due to their *shocking mixture of theological audacity and political thoughtlessness,* to provoke the minds of German citizens."[16] Zahrnt does not differentiate between Barth's various political statements and calls him biased, radical, grandiose, and witty,[17] which are ambivalent adjectives. Barth, he claims, "does actually not know anything about the incarnation of God." In Barth, God "does not really enter history."[18] Barth "cannot be taken as a systematician" but must be taken as a "prophet,"[19] which, of course, is meant in a pejorative sense. The "formalistic exaggeration and artificiality" of the *Church Dogmatics* reveals a "a basic, deeper-lying error" of Barth's theology, namely, its "lack of history" *(Geschichtslosigkeit),* which Zahrnt diagnosed as the "main fault of Barth's entire theology." "In political ethics," this lack of history shows itself in the fact that "Barth, in his description of Christian political decisions and actions shows almost no consideration for the structure of the world."[20] In a one-sided way Zahrnt is fixed upon particularly "extreme" statements of Barth, pulled out of their context from

15. Prolingheuer, *Der Fall*, p. 211. See above, p. 55.

16. Heinz Zahrnt, *Die Sache mit Gott. Die protestantische Theologie im 20. Jahrhundert* (Munich, 1966), p. 225; ET, *The Question of God: Protestant Theology in the Twentieth Century* (London: Collins, 1969), p. 176 (revised) (emphasis by Frank Jehle).

17. Zahrnt, p. 225.

18. Zahrnt, p. 30; ET, pp. 113-14 (revised).

19. Zahrnt, p. 24; ET, p. 92 (revised).

20. Zahrnt, p. 233.

the time of the Romans commentaries. He did not take note of how central the incarnation of God — and with it "The Humanity of God"[21] — is in the *Church Dogmatics*. The phrase "lack of history," in connection with Barth, is incorrect because, according to Barth, God himself enters into history in Christ and submits himself to its conditions. The opinion "that God alone can and must be absolute in contrast to all that is relative, infinite in contrast to all that is finite, exalted in contrast to all that is lowly, active in contrast to all suffering, inviolable in contrast to all temptation, transcendent in contrast to all immanence, and therefore exclusively divine in contrast to everything that is human," is especially, according to the mature Barth, "untenable, corrupt, and pagan."[22] In view of how intensively Barth tried after the Second World War to understand the German people in their concrete structures, it only remains to say: never expect thanks for anything.

In spite of all this, we can see the steadfastness of Barth's friendship with Germany in the fact that, among other things, in the summer semester of 1946 and in the summer semester of 1947, he returned to Bonn, the very place he had been driven out in disgrace in 1935. He presented before many students his *Dogmatics in Outline* and *Christian Doctrine according to the "Heidelberg Catechism."*

---

21. Karl Barth, *Die Menschlichkeit Gottes* (Zürich, 1956).
22. Barth, *KD* IV/1:203; *CD* IV/1:186 (revised).

CHAPTER 10

Between the Eastern and Western Blocs

The political situation and public consciousness changed very rapidly after the Second World War. As a consequence of Yalta, the Soviet Union under Stalin was able to establish a band of dependent and compliant satellite states on its western flank. Only shortly before had National Socialism been the great danger, and already there was confrontation between the Eastern and Western blocs. Many expected that Karl Barth would now raise his voice against Communism as strongly as he did against National Socialism. They were disappointed. Barth did not make a single speech nor did he write a single article along this line. Under the title "How Should This Be Understood?" the Zürich theologian Emil Brunner directed an open letter to Barth in 1948 wherein he insisted that many of his theological fellow travelers had noticed with great displeasure his "position on the political problem of the churches under the Soviet star."[1] An elder in Wattwil, a town in the east of Switzerland, went even further than Brunner, claiming that the "church of Karl Barth" had made a pact "with Communism."[2]

Especially serious, due to the high position of the one who made them, were criticisms of Barth by Markus Feldmann, member of the government of the canton of Bern and Federal Councilor from 1952 on. On September 13, 1950, he declared, before the state parliament of Bern,

1. Barth, *Offene Briefe*, p. 149.
2. Barth, *Offene Briefe*, p. 176.

that representatives of Karl Barth's theology showed, not only a deliberately benevolent neutrality towards Communism," but "an equally deliberate disinterest in the liberal-democratic foundations of our state." Beyond this, Feldmann spoke of a *"noticeable bow that Professor Karl Barth made before Stalin on Sunday, February 6, 1949 in the Münster Church of Bern."*[3] What did Barth *really* say? The following portion of his speech on that Sunday caused a great stir: "It now really makes no sense at all to mention Marxism even for one moment in the same breath with the 'ideology' of the Third Reich, or a man of the stature of Joseph Stalin with such charlatans as Hitler, Göring, Hess, Goebbels, Himmler, Ribbentrop, Rosenberg, Streicher, etc."[4] Reading this passage *today*, we clearly see that Barth overshot the mark with his statement: "a man of the stature of Joseph Stalin." It was a mistake in judgment, and his critics, from Emil Brunner to Markus Feldmann, had every reason to be offended by it. Ever since *The Gulag Archipelago* by Aleksander Solzhenitsyn (published in German in 1974), it has been generally known that Stalin was an unscrupulous dictator. And even in 1949, it could have been known had one remembered the mock trials in Moscow of the 1930s. But the following also has to be considered: Barth was exaggerating rhetorically. Yet anyone who was reading him *carefully* and was not already ill disposed toward him could not possibly have mistaken him for a Stalinist.

Already in 1938, in his famous letter to Josef Hromadka, he had written with regard to the threat of Adolf Hitler that "the possibility of Russian aid" was not a pleasant thought because it would mean "casting out the devil by Beelzebub."[5] Beelzebub, indeed, means devil! There are many other statements of Barth that are aimed in the same direction.

Yet at this point the *entire* passage which contains the unfortunate expression "a man of the stature of Joseph Stalin" should be read:

> [O]ne cannot say about Communism what one had to say ten years ago about National Socialism, namely, that what it means and intends is pure stupidity, the monster of insanity and crime. It now really makes no sense at all to mention Marxism even for one moment in the same breath with the "ideology" of the Third Reich, or a

3. Barth, *Offene Briefe*, p. 220.
4. Barth, "Götze," p. 139; ET, pp. 141-42 (revised).
5. Barth, *Schweizer Stimme*, p. 59. See above, p. 58.

man of the stature of Joseph Stalin with such charlatans as Hitler, Göring, Hess, Goebbels, Himmler, Ribbentrop, Rosenberg, Streicher, etc. What has been tackled in Soviet Russia — albeit with very dirty and bloody hands and in a way that rightly outrages us — is, after all, a constructive idea, the solution of a problem which is a serious and burning problem for us as well, and we with our clean hands have not yet tackled anything like it energetically enough, namely, the social problem. . . . as long as there is still a "freedom" in the West to organize economic crises, a "freedom" to dump our grain into the sea here while people there are starving, so long as such things can happen, we Christians, at least, must refuse to hurl an absolute "No" at the East.[6]

If one reads this text slowly and carefully, it is clear that this was *not*, of course, about justifying Stalinism (much less its horrors). Barth spoke emphatically about the "very dirty and bloody hands" of the Communist regime. But he was of the opinion that with its myth of an Aryan master race and its destructive anti-Semitism, National Socialism did not even have, unlike Marxism, a single good *intention*. An ideology that starts with the thought that representatives of certain peoples and races are *basically* not worthy of living is evil to the core. In Marxism (not in Joseph Stalin) there were at least high ideals in the beginning — primarily in the young Karl Marx as seen in his Paris manuscripts. Marx was rightly outraged over the horrible injustices suffered by the textile workers during the age of early industrialization.

In Marx's main work, *Das Kapital*, we read his description of how at "two, three, four o'clock in the morning . . . children between the ages of nine and ten years are snatched from their dirty beds and forced to earn their basic living, to work until ten, eleven, twelve o'clock at night while their limbs disappear, their bodies shrivel up, their features become dull, and their very humanity freezes into a stone-like torpor, whose mere sight is horrific."[7] Marx sharply analyzed the outrage and developed a model to answer the problems put to him which is worth considering. That Marxism in twentieth-century Russia degenerated into an inhuman system was not in accord with the will of its founder (even though the older Marx revealed certain hardening tendencies). Rosa

6. Barth, "Götze," p. 137; ET, pp. 139-40.

7. Karl Marx, *Das Kapital: Kritik der politischen Ökonomie, 1: Der Produktionsprozess des Kapitals* (Frankfurt am Main and Berlin: Ullstein, 1969), p. 209.

Luxemburg (1870-1919), for instance, showed that it was possible to develop the thoughts of Marx in a different direction than Russia had. At any rate: *the social question truly existed!*

This is what concerned Barth. *For this reason* he refused to treat Marxism and National Socialism as equal. However, Barth's critics in the 1950s failed to see that socialism as it really existed in the Eastern bloc was *not* romantically glorified by him. Shortly before his remark about Stalin which outraged so many at that time, Barth said in the same speech that the kind of Communism ruling in Russia — with its "repulsion and horror" — was showing the world what can be accomplished by "Asian despotism, shrewdness, and ruthlessness."[8] The same attitude of Barth is found in his answer to Emil Brunner in 1948 in which he particularly emphasized that he "did not consider the way of life for the people under Soviet power and the 'people's democracies' affiliated with it as a form of life worthy of our acceptance or approval." It contradicts "our well-founded concepts of justice and freedom." All those who were expecting from him a "political denial" of the system and the methods of Communism could "have it immediately."[9] The Communist system is "nonsense" which is easy to see through (p. 162).

To the elders in Wattwil, Barth wrote on December 23, 1948, that "he did not call Communism a good thing" but what he was against was so many people getting upset about it, "as if it would cost them anything, as if it would make things better or help someone by doing so." He was "against all *fear* of Communism. A people with a clear conscience and with an ordered social and democratic life, have no need to fear it. And much less so a church that was sure of the Gospel of Jesus Christ" (p. 178, emphasis by Frank Jehle).

This attitude was reflected in a letter Barth wrote to a German theologian on October 17, 1950: "Whoever does not [want] Communism — and we all do not want it — should certainly not wage war against it but much rather support serious Socialism!" With respect to Communism, "in the end, there is basically only the positive defence . . . which consists in creating just social conditions acceptable for all layers of the population" (p. 210). Barth was against *cheap* anti-Communism.

8. Barth, "Götze," p. 136; ET, pp. 138-39.
9. Barth, *Offene Briefe*, pp. 163f. The parenthetical page references in the following text are to this work.

In view of imprudent statements made in Switzerland regarding the churches in the Eastern bloc, Barth did not want to apply different standards to different regions in the world. Churches in the Eastern bloc were accused of not being critical enough of their own political system, whereas the same people in the West, as soon as it became an issue for them, had not shown courage either. Such had been the case during the threat of National Socialism. Barth warned against "expecting decisions and steps (or even the lack of them!) from the Hungarian Christians" which we ourselves, if we had to live in the East, "would not dare make" (p. 197).

In the 1950s Communism in Switzerland was for Barth not as great a danger as many believed it to be. As long as harmonious social conditions were ruling in a country, which was the case in Switzerland, there was no need to consider the danger of Communism the most important problem.

In May 1966 the eighty-year-old Barth was asked in a television interview why he had not confronted Communism with such a clear no as he had National Socialism. Barth answered "that he did not live in a Communist country."[10] The danger for the West "is certainly not Communism." Rather the danger that threatens the West is a certain "feeling of well-being" in which man passes through life and is endangered by forgetting the deeper dimensions of life. As for Barth himself, he "did not like to carry logs to a fire that was already burning. Who would not be against Communism?"[11]

On June 3, 1959, Barth said during a conversation in the Zofingia that it was not necessary "to blow the same horn and write articles of condemnation" in a society in which "everyone, as it were, shared the same opinion about Communism." It was different at the "time of National Socialism." Then an "acute danger" existed because many, all over Europe, "had become soft" and were "suggesting that efforts to accommodate" be made because of a "fascination [with National Socialism] or [out] of a fear of being invaded."[12]

On November 18 of that same year, he also made known at the Zofingia that the worst thing was to protest at a time when it did not cost anything and when one did not have to help. In the Second World

10. Barth, *Gespräche* 2, p. 250.
11. Barth, *Gespräche* 2, p. 251.
12. Barth, *Gespräche* 1, p. 11.

War, obsequiousness prevailed "in order not to upset the Germans." This had already been the case in the "conflict of Abyssinia" when, as a result of protests, "economic disadvantages had to be accepted." He, Karl Barth, would "certainly open his mouth if the Russians were to ever stand at Lake Constance (i.e. at the very border of Switzerland)." Though he might perhaps be "the only Swiss" citizen who would do so.[13] This last sentence, of course, was meant in jest.

Until the change in 1989, apologists of Communism (in the East and West) used to argue that the present generation had to make "sacrifices" in order to establish the "perfect" society of the future. You cannot make an omelette without breaking eggs, it was said — a proverb that had been used also in the same context with the human rights offenses of National Socialism. In the summer of 1946 Barth said in opposition to this way of thinking that "man, human dignity, [and] the life of man in the present, may not be trampled upon" for the sake of "the progress and well-being of future generations."[14] Even justice turns into "injustice" wherever it rules in abstract form and does not serve "man's preservation and protection."[15] "Even the most miserable man — certainly not man's egoism, but his humanity — has to be resolutely protected from the autocracy of any mere cause." Man does not have to serve "causes," but causes have "to serve man."[16] These sentences *broadly* denounce the violation of human dignity, even those deriving from a genuinely or disingenuously *good* intention. But they also represent a clear rejection of Stalinism.

Another aspect: though Barth caused offense in the West for not blowing the same horn as the anti-Communists, he spoke a very different language with his friends behind the Iron Curtain. He kept particularly close contact with the Hungarian Reformed Church. In the spring of 1948 he made an extended trip through Hungary. By that time the country was in great danger of falling to Communism (which was to occur a few months later). Before Hungarian students he thought out loud about what form of government would be desirable for a future Hungary. He explained that the future would not be good "if there was no longer room for a federal state under a constitution established by the

---

13. Barth, *Gespräche* 1, p. 51.
14. Barth, *Recht*, p. 65; ET, pp. 171-72 (revised).
15. Barth, *Recht*, pp. 65f.; ET, pp. 171-72.
16. Barth, *Recht*, p. 66; ET, p. 172.

freely educated and freely expressed will of the people, just like the Swiss confederation." "Above all, it would not be good if the Gospel of Jesus Christ, the message of free grace, the word of the Christian, who by faith rules above all things and in love is its servant, would become silent in it."[17] Barth thus took a clear stand here for democracy according to the Swiss model. Freedom of faith and conscience and the right to express diverse opinions was important to him. To oppress free discourse between various political views was completely out of the question.

A particularly basic text is Barth's lecture "The Christian Community in the Midst of Political Change," which he gave in March of 1948 at two different locations in Hungary. From the very beginning he opposed "demonizing, propaganda speech."[18] It was important to him that people have a substantive conversation with each other. It is said that there is "no perfect system of government," yet "there are better and worse systems of government."[19] Those who think about politics from a Christian perspective will always ask: *". . . what will happen to the people . . . ?"*[20] The Christian congregation will "see all persons as human beings and not as wearers of labels, not as mere figures and exponents of a 'cause.'" "I am here not to hate along with the others but to love along with them."[21] The last sentence is a verse from Sophocles' tragedy, *Antigone.*[22] During his trip to Hungary and at other times as well, Barth placed himself conspicuously, as we recall from the previous quotation by Kant,[23] in the tradition of European humanism.

After Barth had spoken (or rather, *had* to speak) in a more abstract way in his lecture "Christian Congregation amid Changing Systems of Government" out of consideration for the difficulty of the political situation in Hungary, he became more concrete in the discussion that followed the lecture. The state must "be supported" by "the free responsibility of the people."[24] The state "could not be put on people's heads like a hat." A just state would be one "in which concepts like order, freedom,

---

17. Barth, *Ungarnreise*, p. 13; ET, p. 60 (revised). See above, p. 5.
18. Barth, *Ungarnreise*, p. 30; ET, p. 77 (revised).
19. Barth, *Ungarnreise*, p. 33; ET, p. 81 (revised).
20. Barth, *Ungarnreise*, p. 45; ET, pp. 92-93 (emphasis by Frank Jehle) (revised).
21. Barth, *Ungarnreise*, p. 46; ET, p. 93 (revised).
22. Sophocles, *Antigone*, l. 523.
23. See above, p. 5.
24. Barth, *Ungarnreise*, pp. 48f.; ET, p. 95 (revised).

fellowship, power, and responsibility" would balance one another. None of these principles could "be made absolute" and rule over the others. "A state in which only the freedom of the individual were valid would not be a constitutional state but a state on its way to becoming an anarchy." If sheer power is predominant in a state, it would not be a "constitutional" state but a "tyrannical" state. "Or if a state wanted simply to establish itself on the principle of community, we would have an ant-like state and not a constitutional state."[25] The last sentence is obviously directed against any excessive nationalism or socialism.

Statements from Barth's 1946 lecture "The Christian Community and the Civil Community" follow the same line. The *civil community*" or the state is "the community of all people of one place, one region, one country." All are essentially bound to each other by a "constitutional system of laws" that is "equally" valid for and binding on them all, and which is defended and maintained by force. The purpose of the state is "the safeguarding of both the external, relative, and provisional *freedom* of individuals and the external, relative, and provisional *peace* of their community and to that extent the safeguarding of the external, relative, and provisional *humanity* of their life . . . as a community." The "three essential forms" in which this safeguarding takes places are the "legislation," the "government and administration," and the "administration of justice."[26] Here again Barth places himself unreservedly in the humanist and Enlightenment tradition, particularly of political liberalism, whose great representatives are Locke (1632-1704), Montesquieu (1689-1755), and Kant (1724-1804). Barth "did not only want to differentiate between the civil community and the Christian community — which means, if carried out onesidedly, [the] surrender of politics to its own laws and the banishment of every single Christian to his own private conscience — rather [he wanted] to point out the analogies between the two."[27] The civil community is "parabolically capable" *(gleichnisfähig)* of "indirectly reflecting the mirror image" of the "truth and reality of the Christian community."[28] For this reason there are within the civil realm, "differences between state and state":

25. Barth, *Ungarnreise,* p. 49; ET, p. 96 (revised).
26. Barth, *Recht,* p. 48; ET, p. 150 (emphasis by F. Jehle) (revised).
27. Heinz Eduard Tödt, "Demokratie I," in *Theologische Realenzyklopädie* 8 (Berlin and New York: de Gruyter, 1981), p. 444.
28. Barth, *Recht,* p. 63; ET, p. 169 (revised).

It would . . . from the perspective of the Church really make no sense to act as if, with respect to the state and to other states, she could find herself in a night in which all cats are grey.[29]

The claim that there is a similarity or dissimilarity between all forms of government and the Gospel is not only well-worn, but wrong. That one can go to hell in a democracy and be saved during mob-rule or in a dictatorship is true. But it is not true that as a Christian one can just as seriously support, want, and strive for mob-rule or a dictatorship as for democracy.[30]

There is indeed an affinity between the Christian community and the civil community of *free* peoples![31]

Barth was asked in Hungary how a Christian should behave with regard to a state which pays no attention to justice, a state which is "perhaps" a godless state, a state which would show itself "sooner or later to be an enemy of the church because of its worldview."[32] Barth first called to mind in this context Acts 5:29: "We must obey God rather than men," and added: "in such a situation the main thing for us Christians is to keep calm and not lose our sense of humor." The question: "May one join a party in order to keep one's job?" — which was in reference to being forced into membership of the Communist party in order to have a career — was answered by Barth with a clear no. It was not "recommended" to go against one's own conscience. At this point there was not "a Yes and a No" but "only a No." It is "not good to walk around with a broken conscience."[33]

Barth's attitude toward Communism becomes especially clear in his correspondence with the Hungarian theologian Albert Bereczky. Originally Barth felt great personal regard for this man who, in the summer of 1944, fought to rescue Hungarian Jews.[34] With guarded reservation Barth supported the plan in 1948 to appoint Bereczky bishop of the Reformed Hungarians. However, over the years it became more and more clear that Bereczky completely identified with the Communist system in

29. Barth, *Recht,* p. 20; ET, p. 119 (revised).
30. Barth, *Recht,* pp. 41f.; ET, pp. 144-45 (revised).
31. Barth, *Recht,* p. 74; ET, p. 182 (revised).
32. Barth, *Ungarnreise,* pp. 50f.; ET, p. 97 (revised).
33. Barth, *Ungarnreise,* p. 51; ET, pp. 98-99 (revised).
34. Busch, *Bogen,* p. 516.

Hungary. He had been a member of the head committee of the Ecumenical Council of Churches since 1948. He tried in this capacity to stop declarations of the World Council of Churches against the East and at the same time tried to persuade it to take positions against the West.

Bereczky's sympathy for Communism was expressed by his statement "that the God who formed world history" wanted to establish through socialism (by which he meant Communism) a "new and just order of human life together." "Christian churchmen of the West" had to recognize that it was a "sin" to hold on to the political system of the West. This system had already been "judged" by God and therefore "belonged to the past."[35]

At this point (which, for Markus Feldmann, would have been important information) Barth became furious. In a private letter — not intended to be made public in the West (or East) — Barth wrote Bereczky that he "was about to enter into a serious *theological error.*" He was in the process of making "his agreement with Communism into a part of the Christian message and into an article of faith." And this article of faith was "eclipsing all others," as always happens when such "strange doctrines" are introduced (p. 279). With the deliberately chosen phrase "strange doctrine," Barth was recalling Barmen and the Church Struggle in Germany.[36] He said, furthermore, that Bereczky was interpreting "the entire Credo and the entire Bible" with this new article of faith. In other words, he was beginning to enter "into the *ideological*-Christian way of thinking which at one time, under different circumstances, had been the way of the 'German Christians'" (p. 279, emphasis by Jehle). How did he know "about 'the great things' that 'the God who was forming world history was to do on earth through Socialism' anyway" (p. 281)?

> Is there then no other way in Reformed Hungary but to work every time in such total agreement with the regime ruling at the time? (p. 282)

> Is it not right that we here — your friends [in the West!] — are swimming *against our* stream while you so constantly swim *with yours?* And for almost six years now! (p. 283)

35. Barth, *Offene Briefe,* p. 280. The parenthetical page references in the following text are to this work.
36. See above, pp. 13-14 and 53-54.

Barth's rebuke of Bereczky was by no means an exception. The Czech theologian Josef L. Hromadka — to whom Barth, in the fall of 1938, had sent his famous letter on armed resistance against Germany[37] — also developed tendencies (similar to Bereczky) that were friendly toward Communism *after* the Second World War. He saw in the Russian Revolution of 1917 an "event of salvation." Barth now supported the oppressed Protestant Church in Czechoslovakia. He did not usually publicly contradict Hromadka, whom he, personally, highly regarded, in spite of his political "affiliation." But in this case as well, a personal and not public letter during Christmas of 1962 reveals Barth's criticisms of Hromadka. This important letter is quoted almost in its entirety because Barth's position becomes particularly clear here:

> Dear Joseph, . . . in your latest essay [on the Cuban crisis of 1962] it struck me almost like a blow: in its negative mode, there is the lack of any higher place above the clouds of ideologies, interests, and forces which confront and conflict with one another in the cold war; and in its positive mode, there is the arbitrariness with which you not only champion one of the fronts personally but also expect the church and the world to do the same. Evangelically, what I regard as right and even commanded in the modern situation is . . . that our attitude should be one in which, with our Word and for the sake of God, we can be in helpful solidarity with man as such, and therefore with those of the left and the right, those who suffer and those who strive, the righteous and the unrighteous, Christians and atheists, the followers of humanisms A, B, C, and D. What I see you doing when your theology — as it should — becomes political is something different: you pressure us and other contemporaries with the demand that we should discover the newly developing world of freedom and peace represented in the figures of Nikita [Khrushchev], Mao [Tse-tung], and even Fidel [Castro], and see in the figure of John [F. Kennedy] an incarnation of the old social and political order that has been outdated since 1917 and is now crumbling away. My hair stands on end at this black and white depiction and the demand that we should adopt it.
>
> I will not quarrel about the concrete political tasks that you . . . set

37. See above, p. 58.

97

in your essay, although I have various reservations and amendments in relation to each of them. This would lead to a political discussion that cannot be our purpose. It is rather a question of the method and style of your presentation, in view of which I cannot suppress my old suspicion, familiar enough to you, that your attitudes and corresponding Christian admonitions are determined entirely by a point of view which is materially identical with that of one Leviathan that is striving for power today, except that, and this is very important, for you this point of view is undergirded by a reference to Jesus Christ and Holy Scripture, though I cannot see it. Dear Joseph, do you not realize that Emil Brunner, Reinhold Niebuhr, and other western fathers defend their western outlook with the same method and in the same style, and being able to do this they bring on the scene their crusade against communism, so that you and they are waging the "cold war" in just the same way? . . . How shall we then . . . , as long as such declarations are coming from you, make it clear to the Christian and secular world on this side of the iron curtain that the issue for us (and basically for you, too, is it not?) is neither an anti-communist peace nor a communist peace but the peace of God that surpasses all understanding — and therefore justice (in the biblical sense of the word) both against all and for all?[38]

This great letter shows what *really* concerned Barth, perhaps even more clearly than the shorter one to Bereczky. To put it negatively, he was certainly not interested in supporting Communism or Stalinism! Even *before* his letter to Hromadka, Barth had made a critical statement during a conversation at the Schaffhausen Pastors' Convention, saying that Hromadka's views represented "a particular kind of philosophy of history." In 1933 the "German Christians" had talked "just like that" in Germany.[39] If one recalls how fundamentally Barth rejected the "German Christians" at that time, it is clear that he did not make it easy on his friend in the East, Josef L. Hromadka, either.

For Barth it was important that one not orient oneself one-sidedly in preaching in the name of Jesus Christ to the politically (and economi-

---

38. Rohkrämer, *Briefwechsel*, pp. 213ff. ET, *Karl Barth, Letters, 1961-1968*, trans. Geoffrey W. Bromiley (Grand Rapids: Eerdmans, 1981), pp. 82-83 (slightly revised).
39. Barth, *Gespräche 1*, p. 393.

cally) powerful. Often, but not always, it was about swimming against the stream. During his visit to Hungary in the spring of 1948, he asserted "that Christians could probably show their gratitude for God's gift and order, even in the best of states, only in the form of serious opposition."[40] The "political *co-responsibility* of the church," particularly if it is "serious," could "never be uncritical participation." Christians would not be "the easiest citizens to get along with, neither for a government nor for a powerful majority or minority, neither for a clique nor for an individual personality."[41] "Christian politics would always have to remain for the world a strange, obscure, and surprising matter," or else it would "certainly not be Christian politics."[42]

These statements tell us something about Karl Barth. During the decades of his active participation in politics, there were always new surprises. It was always a *critical* (which means a discriminating) participation in politics, a basis for nonconformism in the Christian faith. Barth did not strive for a "Christian state." But the Christian faith was for him a life-sustaining enzyme[43] in the liberal state.

---

40. Barth, *Ungarnreise*, p. 34; ET, p. 81 (revised).
41. Barth, *Ungarnreise*, p. 34; ET, p. 82 (revised).
42. Barth, *Ungarnreise*, p. 45; ET, p. 92 (revised).
43. I owe this most appropriate formulation to Prof. Dr. Roland Kley, St. Gallen.

CHAPTER 11

Karl Barth's Political Ethics

Karl Barth lived for almost eighty-three years. For his generation he lived a long life, and was allowed to remain active almost to the end. Even on the night before his death he worked on a lecture he wanted to give in January of 1969 in Zürich on the occasion of the Ecumenical Week of Prayer for the Unity of Christendom, entitled "Starting Out, Turning Round, Confessing."[1] There were always new starts in Barth's life — theological and political ones.

Considering the individual chapters of this book, one notices many constants in Barth's life which form a well-rounded whole. The first constant is his facing of the world and his alertness. Barth was not an introverted scholar who withdrew into the proverbial ivory tower in order to devote himself to playing with glass beads. The most important reading material for him, next to the Bible, was the newspaper. The political knowledge of the not-even-twenty-year-old theology student as well as the over-eighty-year-old man is most impressive.

Another constant is that his interest in the world was always combined with critical engagement. Barth did not withhold his personal opinions regarding relevant questions of the day. He expressed them in an undisguised manner. Wherever he had the opportunity, he tried to intervene in the world and change it in ways he saw as positive. Barth was a difficult contemporary. He always anew swam against the stream.

1. Barth, *Letzte Zeugnisse*, pp. 61-71; ET, pp. 51-60.

The theological beginner as well as the famous professor was often distinguished by the minority position he took. He never said what others wanted to hear.

Probably many "Zofingers" in 1906 thought their fraternity brother was carrying his social engagement a bit too far. (Eduard von Steiger was among that group.) Between 1933 and 1935, it was a bitter experience for Barth that, in the end, even his friends in the Confessing Church left him out in the cold. A presentation of the events in Switzerland during the Second World War sounds more harmless today than it was at the time. It was an unpleasant experience to have one's phone tapped and to be banned from speaking politically. The time of the Cold War was similar to it. One did not have an easy life resisting the prevailing mood of anti-Communism.

Another red thread that runs throughout Barth's entire life's work is — in the expression made popular by the New Testament Professor Ernst Käsemann — the "eschatological proviso" under which all his political (and theological) statements stood. Barth was not a "totalitarian" thinker. In his lecture in the spring of 1933, "The First Commandment as Theological Axiom," he very seriously said that since every human work is dependent upon the forgiveness of sins, "arguments in theology, even good and necessary arguments . . . could only be held in penultimate fashion and by no means in absolute seriousness and anger." After that which is necessary had been said, "the 'bond of peace' (Eph. 4:3) would also have to become visible." The necessary theological argument can only be held "in common hope."[2] These sentences are all the more remarkable because they were spoken at a time of most intense theological and political debate.

The *fundamental distinction between the "last" and the "next to the last"* became world renowned through Dietrich Bonhoeffer[3] — mainly because he emphasized several times in his letters from prison that "we cannot say the last word before we say the next to the last." "We live in the next to the last and believe the last."[4] This distinction is already found in Barth's Romans commentaries, and it is the tacit prerequisite of

2. Barth, *Fragen und Antw.*, p. 143.

3. Dietrich Bonhoeffer, *Ethik*, ed. Eberhard Bethge (Munich, 1963), pp. 128ff.; *Widerstand und Ergebung* (Munich, 1970), p. 459 (index).

4. Bonhoeffer, *Widerstand und Ergebung*, p. 176.

all his political interventions. Ever anew, the warning against absolutism and dogmatism occurs.

When he entered the Social Democratic Party in January 1915, he knew himself only obliged "to faith in the Greatest," that is, to faith in God "which does not exclude but rather includes work and suffering in a realm which is not yet complete."[5]

Regarding his practical work on behalf of the workers in Safenwil, he said: "I am doing it without enthusiasm, simply because it is necessary."[6] Or, as he said in his old age, with deliberately reserved and sober words: "In Safenwil my main interest in Socialism was the problem of the labor union movement."[7]

During the period of the Romans commentaries, he said: "[The Christian] sheds all pathos, all lack of restraint, and unbrokenness."[8] The state should be "starved religiously."[9] One should fulfill "one's duty as a citizen and party member with a cool mind and without any illusions."[10] Politics *becomes a possibility* where the essential competitive character of this matter is obvious and from that moment on where the note of 'absoluteness' has vanished from both thesis and antithesis in order to make room for human possibilities which are perhaps moderately intended or perhaps radically intended."[11] Although it was a misunderstanding, it was perhaps no coincidence that some in Germany in the 1920s believed they heard a call to political abstinence in Barth's Romans commentaries.

During the time of National Socialism it was also obvious that, precisely *for that reason*, Barth could not possibly sympathize with Hitler because he wanted to remain sober and nonideological — just like "the chanting of the hours by the Benedictines in Maria Laach, which would go on undoubtedly without break or interruption according to its order even in the Third Reich."[12]

Back in Switzerland, Barth was one of the most decisive champions

---

5. See above, p. 28.
6. See above, p. 31.
7. See above, p. 36.
8. See above, p. 41.
9. See above, p. 41.
10. See above, p. 42.
11. See above, p. 44.
12. See above, pp. 13 and 46.

of an uncompromising resistance against National Socialism. Yet he also mocked every Swiss "folk ideology" and every Swiss national "myth."

After the war, Barth was against an ideological anti-Communism and *at the same time* against a Christian glorification of Communism in the East. He fought in both directions against an absolutism and a theologization of political positions which were intrinsically secular.

In retrospect, Barth said much later:

> I myself am . . . liberal — and perhaps even more liberal than those who call themselves liberals on this field. . . . True liberality must consist in speaking and thinking in responsibility and openness to all sides, backward and forward, in the past and in the future, in which — may I say so — one is entirely modest. "Modest" does not mean sceptical but it means that one is aware of this: whatever I am thinking and saying now will also have its limits. This does not hinder me, however, from saying very decisively that which I think I see and recognize![13]

Here, at almost the end of this book, a further question must be addressed. For a long time it has been common practice to emphasize the far-reaching difference between Barth and Luther with respect to political ethics: Barth's political ethics is often deemed the *doctrine of "Christ's royal reign"* in contrast to the so-called *two-kingdom doctrine* of Luther. I consider this distinction somewhat skewed, and for this reason not very helpful. The following shall clarify its meaning:

The *doctrine of "Christ's royal reign"* begins with the fact that Christian faith lives by the assurance of the victory of the crucified Christ which has been revealed in his resurrection. On this basis all Christians are now called "to join in carrying out the victory of Christ in obedient discipleship. Such action expresses itself [particularly well] in the undivided co-responsibility of Christians and the church in shaping all areas of life, including, therefore, the state."[14] What is particularly striking about this doctrine is its "criticism of autonomous laws of the State and the privatization of the Christian faith."[15] Often the second thesis of the Theological Declaration of Barmen of 1934 is quoted:

13. Barth, *Gespräche* 2, pp. 544f.
14. Christian Walther, "Königsherrschaft Christi," in *Theologische Realenzyklopädie* 19 (Berlin and New York, 1990), p. 314.
15. Walther, p. 315.

As Jesus Christ is God's assurance of the forgiveness of all our sins, so in the same way and with the same seriousness he is also God's mighty claim upon our whole life. Through him befalls us a joyful deliverance from the godless fetters of this world for a free, grateful service to his creatures.

We reject the false doctrine, as though there were areas of our life in which we would not belong to Jesus Christ, but to other lords — areas in which we would not need justification and sanctification through him.[16]

The point here is that the claim of Christ's rule is "upon our whole life."

For Luther[17] himself, the starting point for his two-kingdom doctrine (which only in the twentieth century was named as such and, remarkably, by of all people, Karl Barth)[18] is the question of how Jesus' Sermon on the Mount must be understood, for example, in Matthew 5:39: "But I say to you, Do not resist one who is evil. But if someone strikes you on the right cheek, turn to him the other also." The classical Roman Catholic tradition says here, to put it in a rather simplistic way, that for average Christian people it is enough to respect the Ten Commandments. Nonviolence (the turning of the other cheek), poverty, chastity, and obedience are, on the other hand, an additional opportunity for Christian elites (the disciples of Christ in the more narrow sense of this word) who first of all follow these "evangelical counsels" in the monasteries and hermitages.

Luther had a different perspective on the relationship between the Sermon on the Mount and the Ten Commandments. There are not different kinds of Christians; rather, before God, all are the same and all have to submit to the same principles. For me, as a "Christian person," the absolute commandment is valid in every situation. I may never defend only myself. "Suffering! suffering! Cross! cross! This and nothing else is the Christian law!"[19] as Luther called out to the rebellious peasants in the midst of the Peasants' War of 1525.

16. Book of Confessions, p. 257.

17. This passage is an adaptation of Frank Jehle's "Du darfst kein riesiges Maul sein, das alles gierig in sich hineinfrisst und verschlingt." *Freiburger Vorlesungen über die Wirtschaftsethik der Reformatoren Luther, Zwingli und Calvin* (Basel: Gotthelf Verlag, 1996), pp. 29ff.

18. Martin Honecker, *Grundriss der Sozialethik* (Berlin and New York, 1995), p. 14.

19. Luther, "Admonition to Peace," LW 46, p. 29.

But for myself, *as "an officeholder"* (for instance, as a father or mother, a mayor, judge, or prince, or also as the owner of a company), I am obligated, not for myself but certainly on behalf of those entrusted to me, to fight against the evil in the world, and if necessary, even with violence.

According to Luther, every Christian is a citizen of two worlds, the kingdom of God on the right and the kingdom of God on the left. In the realm on the right hand of God, Christ himself reigns through Word and Sacrament. Here the instructions of the Sermon on the Mount are valid. In the realm on the left hand of God (here, of course, God is also ultimately reigning, which really has to be considered), the emperor rules with the sword.[20] In this realm there are no absolute norms but only relative ones. In this area of relative norms, justice and fairness shall reign — and not unconditional love. Luther's "doctrine of two Kingdoms [was] a serious attempt to theologically justify Christian existence in the midst of the reality of the world."[21]

Among several more recent Lutheran writers, this two-kingdom doctrine has been significantly modified. While for Luther it was obvious that God also reigned in the kingdom on his left — and for this reason his commandments had to be followed here as well — the idea of so-called "autonomous laws" was developed, that is, the notion that politics, law, economy, science, and art each follow their own laws. The gospel and the church may not interfere. Important representatives of this new perspective on Luther were Christoph Ernst Luthardt and Friedrich Naumann. In their books, *Die Ethik Luthers in ihren Grundzügen* (1875) and *Briefe über die Religion* (1903), they made a distinction between the "inwardness" of faith and the outward dimensions of the secular, "autonomous laws," and thus dualistically separated them from each other.[22] For decades debate over this two-kingdom doctrine has complicated the discussion and made it very problematic.

But it would be misleading if it were claimed that an all too deep chasm existed between Karl Barth and the original, correctly understood two-kingdom doctrine of Martin Luther. Luther himself did "not yet

20. *Die Religion in Geschichte und Gegenwart* 6, 3rd ed. (Tübingen: J. C. B. Mohr, 1962), pp. 1945ff. (Franz Lau).

21. Walther von Loewenich, *Martin Luther. Der Mann und das Werk*, 3rd ed. (Munich: List Verlag, 1962), p. 227.

22. Honecker, p. 25.

know of an autonomous law of the world, politics, and economics exempt from the law of God."[23] Exactly as in Barth, the purpose of Luther's two-kingdom doctrine was nothing more and nothing less than for a politics and economics free of ideology. *Politics is the art of the possible and not the establishment of God's kingdom on earth.* According to Gerhard Ebeling, today's leading Luther scholar, it is one of the "most trivial distortions" of the two-kingdom doctrine to suggest that by it "the world is released from its dependence upon God and faith from responsibility to the world."[24] There is no actual contradiction between the "real" Luther and Barth's statement in the Theological Declaration of Barmen that there are no "areas of our life in which we would not belong to Jesus Christ, but to other lords." But Luther as well as Barth knew very well — and it was essential for them — how to distinguish between the "last" and the "next to the last." *This distinction can be understood as a creative development of the original two-kingdom doctrine of Martin Luther.* It does not make any sense to rashly play Barth and Luther off against each other (although both of them did, of course, not teach exactly the same things, which also has to do with the fact that they lived in two different centuries).

After his discussion with Lutherans like Paul Althaus and others (though not with Luther himself), Barth increasingly emphasized the main features of his political ethics differently. Apart from his lecture "Gospel and Law" (1935), two other lectures are important: "Justification and Justice" of 1938 and "The Christian Community and the Civil Community" of 1946. These lectures have been cited several times. Among other things it was said that the civil community has the potential of "not directly but *indirectly* reflecting the *mirror image*"[25] of the truth and reality of the Christian community. In the Theological Declaration of Barmen, Barth formulated these famous sentences about the Christian community: "The Christian Church is the *congregation of brethren*. . . . The various offices in the Church do not establish a *dominion of some over the others;* on the contrary, they are for the exercise of the ministry entrusted to and enjoined upon the whole congregation."[26]

With this background, it is clear that Barth preferred democracy as a

23. Honecker, p. 26.
24. Gerhard Ebeling, *Wort und Glaube III* (Tübingen: J. C. B. Mohr, 1975), pp. 575f.
25. See above, p. 93.
26. Book of Confessions, pp. 257f. (emphasis by F. Jehle).

form of government over other forms of government, although he was thoroughly sober about it and did not idealize it. Analogically, democracy nevertheless reflects the way Christians have to deal with each other. Uncontrolled and unlimited "power of some over the others" is, from a Christian theological point of view, an absurdity. There are statements found throughout Barth's works that claim that "basically everyone" is "responsible for the actions of the state."[27] If possible, a "federal constitutional state like the Swiss confederation" should be striven for and founded upon the "freely educated and freely expressed will of the people."[28] "The claim that there is a similarity or dissimilarity between all forms of government and the Gospel is not only well-worn, but wrong."[29] "There is indeed an affinity between the Christian community and the civil community of free peoples!"[30] It was mentioned in the introduction that Barth had for this reason an especially high regard for the British political system.[31] In his lecture "Our Church and Switzerland in the Present Time," given in November of 1940, Barth made an important statement about the term "democracy." He said it is unfortunate that there is not a better word available for that form of government which seems most appropriate. For "ruling" could and should, strictly speaking, "not be done by 'the people' but by the justice and duty of fellowship and freedom."[32]

Finally, this is another basic theological thought regarding the theme of Christian faith and politics that was important to Barth which he therefore took up in several contexts. Barth noticed that an essential feature in the New Testament and in the ancient church is the fact that many members of the early Christian church refused to sacrifice before the statue of the Roman emperor. When they were forced to do so, they chose martyrdom. *But they were praying for the emperor!* Barth derived from this that it contradicts the basic thought of Christianity to see in the state — even in the best of states — something absolute. Even the best state is relative. The state may not be "worshiped." But the most important service that Christians can render to the state is prayer. And who-

---

27. See above, p. 4.
28. See above, pp. 5 and 91-92.
29. See above, p. 94.
30. See above, p. 94.
31. See above, p. 4.
32. Barth, *Schweizer Stimme*, p. 165.

ever is praying for the state will spontaneously meet it not passively or indifferently. *To pray for someone or something means the most intensive participation possible.* I cannot pray for something if I am not at the same time ready to participate in it and to — where the possibility arises for me — commit myself to it.

In his previously cited lecture, "Justification and Justice," of 1938, Barth said that the "prayer for the bearers of authority in the state" is part of the "basic rations" of the church's existence.[33] This is "fundamentally and comprehensively" the "work of the church for the state."[34] After the war, in his 1946 lecture "The Christian Community and the Civil Community," he stated this theological insight more pointedly: the Christian community prays "for the civil community." But as she is praying for it, she "takes up responsibility for it before God. And she would not do this seriously if she would only pray and not also, while praying for it, work actively for it."[35] To repeat the quotation cited at the beginning of an earlier chapter: "A silent community, merely observing the events of the time, would not be a Christian community."[36] This is the legacy of Karl Barth's political ethics.

33. Barth, *Recht,* p. 29; ET, p. 130.
34. Barth, *Recht,* p. 34; ET, p. 136 (revised).
35. Barth, *Recht,* p. 55; ET, p. 159 (revised).
36. See above, p. 79.

BIBLIOGRAPHY

Beintker, Michael. "Karl Barth." In *Religion in Geschichte und Gegenwart, Vierte*, pp. 1138-41. Wholly new revised edition. Vol. 1. Tübingen: J. C. B. Mohr, 1998.

Jüngel, Eberhard. "Karl Barth." In *Theologische Realenzyklopädie*, 5:251-68. Berlin and New York: de Gruyter, 1980.

Since 1971 the Theologischer Verlag Zürich has been publishing the *Gesamtausgabe* of Karl Barth's works, which gives access to his entire literary work. These volumes are designated in the following with "GA."

Karl Barth's Main Writings

Dogm. im Entwurf
> *Die christliche Dogmatik im Entwurf.* Vol. 1 of *Die Lehre vom Worte Gottes. Prolegomena zur christlichen Dogmatik.* 1927. Edited by Gerhard Sauter. Zürich, 1982 (GA 14).

Ethik I
> *Ethik I.* Academic lectures in Münster, summer term 1928, repeated in Bonn, summer term 1930. Edited by Dietrich Braun. Zürich, 1973 (GA 2). ET, *Ethics.* Translated by Geoffrey W. Bromiley. New York: Seabury Press, 1981.

Ethik II

Ethik II. Academic lectures in Münster, summer term 1928/29, repeated in Bonn, winter term 1930/31. Edited by Dietrich Braun. Zürich: Theologischer Verlag Zürich, 1978 (GA 10). ET, *Ethics*. Translated by Geoffrey W. Bromiley. New York: Seabury Press, 1981.

Fragen und Antw.

Theologische Fragen und Antworten. In *Gesammelte Vorträge*, vol. 3 (1927-42). 2nd ed. Zürich: Theologischer Verlag, 1986.

Gifford Lectures

Gotteserkenntnis und Gottesdienst nach reformatorischer Lehre. 20 Vorlesungen über das Schottische Bekenntnis von 1560 gehalten an der Universität Aberdeen im Frühjahr 1937 und 1938. Zollikon, 1938. ET, *The Knowledge of God and the Service of God according to the Teaching of the Reformation: Recalling the Scottish Confession of 1560, the Gifford Lectures Delivered in the University of Aberdeen in 1937 and 1938*. Translated by J. L. M. Haire and Ian Henderson. New York: Charles Scribner's Sons, 1939.

"Götze"

"Der Götze wackelt." In *Zeitkritische Aufsätze, Reden und Briefe von 1930 bis 1960*, edited by Karl Kupisch. Berlin, 1961. ET, "The Church between East and West." Translated by Stanley Godman. In *Against the Stream: Shorter Post-War Writings, 1946-1952*. London: SCM Press, 1954.

Grundriss

Dogmatik im Grundriss. Vorlesungen gehalten im Sommersemester 1946 an der Universität Bonn im Sommersemester 1947. 8th ed. Zürich: Theologischer Verlag, 1998. ET, *Dogmatics in Outline*. Translated by G. T. Thomson. London: SCM Press, 1949.

Heidelb. Kat.

Die christliche Lehre nach dem Heidelberger Katechismus. Academic lectures delivered at the University of Bonn in the summer term of 1947. Zollikon-Zürich: Evangelischer Verlag, 1948. ET, *The Heidelberg Catechism for Today*. Translated by Shirley C. Guthrie, Jr. London: Epworth Press, 1964.

KD

Die kirchliche Dogmatik. Munich, Zollikon, and Zürich, 1932ff. ET, *Church Dogmatics.* Edited by G. W. Bromiley and T. F. Torrance. Edinburgh: T. & T. Clark, 1956-75.

Kl. Arbeiten 1

Vorträge und kleinere Arbeiten 1905-1909. Edited by Hans-Anton Drewes and Hinrich Stoevesandt in collaboration with Herbert Helms. Zürich: Theologischer Verlag Zürich, 1992 (GA 21).

Kl. Arbeiten 2

Vorträge und kleinere Arbeiten 1909-1914. Edited by Hans-Anton Drewes and Hinrich Stoevesandt in collaboraton with Herbert Helms and Friedrich-Wilhelm Marquardt. Zürich: Theologischer Verlag, 1993 (GA 22).

Kl. Arbeiten 3

Vorträge und kleinere Arbeiten 1922-1925. Edited by Holger Finze. Zürich: Theologischer Evangelischer Verlag, 1990 (GA 19).

Letzte Zeugnisse

Letzte Zeugnisse. Zürich: Theologischer Verlag, 1969. ET, *Final Testimonies.* Translated by Geoffrey W. Bromiley. Grand Rapids: Eerdmans, 1977.

Pred. 1921-1935

Predigten 1921-1935. Edited by Holger Finze. Zürich: Theologischer Verlag Zürich, 1998 (GA 31).

Prot. Theologie

Die Protestantische Theologie im 19. Jahrhundert. 6th ed. Zürich, 1994. ET, *Protestant Theology in the Nineteenth Century.* Translated by Brian Cozens and John Bowden. Grand Rapids: Eerdmans, 2002.

Recht

Rechtfertigung und Recht, Christengemeinde und Bürgergemeinde, Evangelium und Gesetz. Zürich: Theologischer Verlag, 1998. ET, *Community, State, and Church.* Gloucester, Mass.: Peter Smith, 1968.

Römerbrief 1

Der Römerbrief (Erste Fassung). 1919. Edited by Hermann Schmidt. Zürich, 1985 (GA 16).

Römerbrief 2

Der Römerbrief. 15th printing of the new revision. Zürich, 1999. Listed are the page numbers of the original edition; the page numbers in parentheses are those of the fifteenth reprint.

Schweizer Stimme

Eine Schweizer Stimme 1938-1945. 3rd ed. Zürich: Theologischer Verlag Zürich, 1985.

Ungarnreise

Christliche Gemeinde im Wechsel der Staatsordnungen. Dokumente einer Ungarnreise 1948. Zollikon: Evangelischer Verlag, 1948. ET, "The Christian Community in the Midst of Political Change: Documents of a Hungarian Journey." Translated by Mrs. E. M. Delacour and Stanley Godman. In Against the Stream: Shorter Post-War Writings, 1946-1952. London: SCM Press, 1954.

Conversations, Letters, Documentations as well as Biographical and Historical Presentations

Barth, *Gedenkfeier*

Barth, Karl. Karl Barth 1886-1968. Gedenkfeier im Basler Münster. Zürich: Theologischer Verlag Zürich, 1969.

Barth, *Gespräche* 1

Barth, Karl. Gespräche 1959-1962. Edited by Eberhard Busch. Zürich: Theologischer Verlag Zürich, 1995 (GA 25).

Barth, *Gespräche* 2

Barth, Karl. Gespräche 1964-1968. Edited by Eberhard Busch. Zürich, 1997 (GA 28).

Bibliography

Barth, *Offene Briefe*

Barth, Karl. *Offene Briefe 1945-1968.* Edited by Diether Koch. Zürich: Theologischer Verlag Zürich, 1984 (GA 15).

Barth-Rade

Karl Barth–Martin Rade. Ein Briefwechsel. With an introduction and edited by Christoph Schwöbel. Gütersloh, 1981.

Barth-Thurneysen

Karl Barth–Eduard Thurneysen. Briefwechsel, Band 1. 1913-1921. Revised and edited by Eduard Thurneysen. Zürich: Theologischer Verlag Zürich, 1973 (GA 3).

Book of Confessions

The Constitution of the Presbyterian Church (U.S.A.). Part 1: Book of Confessions. Published by the Office of the General Assembly, Louisville, KY, 1994.

Busch, *Bogen*

Busch, Eberhard. *Unter dem Bogen des einen Bundes. Karl Barth und die Juden 1933-1945.* Neukirchen-Vluyn: Neukirchener Verlag, 1996.

Busch, *Lebenslauf*

Busch, Eberhard. *Karl Barths Lebenslauf.* Munich: Chr. Kaiser Verlag, 1975. ET, *Karl Barth: His Life from Letters and Autobiographical Texts.* Translated by John Bowden. Philadelphia: Fortress, 1976.

Busch, *Reformationstag*

Busch, Eberhard, ed. *Reformationstag 1933. Dokumente der Begegnung Karl Barths mit dem Pfarrernotbund in Berlin.* Zürich: Theologischer Verlag Zürich, 1998.

Fürst, *Scheidung*

Fürst, Walter, ed. *"Dialektische Theologie" in Scheidung und Bewährung 1933-1936.* Theologische Bücherei 34. Munich, 1966. ET, *Theological Existence To-day!* Translated by R. Birch Hoyle. London: Hodder and Stoughton, 1933.

Moltmann, *Anfänge*

Moltmann, Jürgen, ed. *Anfänge der dialektischen Theologie, Teil 1.* Karl Barth, Heinrich Barth, Emil Brunner. Theologische Bücherei 17/I. 5th ed. Munich, 1985.

Prolingheuer, *Der Fall*

Prolingheuer, Hans. *Der Fall Karl Barth 1934-1935.* Neukirchen-Vluyn: Neukirchener Verlag, 1977.

Rohkrämer, *Briefwechsel*

Rohkrämer, Martin, ed. *Freundschaft im Widerspruch. Der Briefwechsel zwischen Karl Barth, Josef L. Hromadka und Josef B. Soucek 1935-1968.* With an introduction by Jan Milic Lochman. Zürich, 1995.

Scholder, *Die Kirchen 1*

Scholder, Klaus. *Die Kirchen und das Dritte Reich.* Vol. 1. Frankfurt am Main, Berlin, and Vienna, 1977. ET, *The Church and the Third Reich, I: 1918-1934.* Translated by John Bowden. Philadelphia: Fortress, 1988.

Scholder, *Die Kirchen 2*

Scholder, Klaus. *Die Kirchen und das Dritte Reich.* Vol. 2. Berlin, 1985. ET, *The Church and the Third Reich, II: The Year of Disillusionment 1934, Barmen and Rome.* Translated by John Bowden. Philadelphia: Fortress, 1988.

Schuster, *Quellenbuch*

Schuster, Hermann, and others, eds. *Quellenbuch zur Kirchengeschichte III.* 8th ed. Frankfurt am Main, Berlin, Bonn, and Munich: Diesterweg, 1968.

INDEX OF NAMES